The Millionaire Machine

Books by William L. Atwood

The Lottery Solution

The Lottery Solution – Revised and Enlarged Edition

The Millionaire Machine

by

William L. Atwood

RIVERCROSS PUBLISHING, INC.
Orlando

ISBN: 1-58141-020-4

Library of Congress Catalog Card Number:00-059082

First Printing

Library of Congress Cataloging-in-Publication Data

Atwood, William L.
   The millionaire machine / by William L. Atwood.
      p.cm.
   ISBN 1-58141-020-4
    1.   Finance, Personal. 2. Investments. I. Title.

HG179 .A88 2000
332.024'01 - - dc21

                                        00-059082

Dedication

I am dedicating this book to Christian Kan. When I told her the idea; she asked, "Can you make common people into millionaires?" Just seconds later she exclaimed, "You can make common people into millionaires!" Yes, Chris. In time all things are possible. I believe we can reduce the time element enough for many to become millionaires, or at least financially independent. Christian saw it before I did and she is the nicest person I know.

Special thanks to Mark and Cindy. A painting in their living room called, "Justification for Higher Education," has certainly contributed to the spirit of this book. The painting depicts a waterfront Mediterranean style house in the background. The foreground has a five-car garage with five cars parked in it: a Mercedes, a Corvette, a Porsche, a Ferrari, and a BMW. For anyone wanting a million it's an inspiration!

I am grateful to Minitab, Inc., 3081 Enterprise Drive, State College, PA 16801-3008 for the use of their statistical software.

Table of Contents

A Note about Discrimination:

I have just read an article in one of the financial magazines. This article states that black women are not receiving their fair share of market revenues. The reasons mentioned include lower earnings, family expenses, cultural values, education on investing, and lack of access to necessary information. Many of these reasons result from discrimination. Years ago the market consisted of rich white men selling to rich white men. Today the middle class has come into the market with mutual funds, IRAs, 401(k)'s and other tax-deferred plans.

The reason black women don't make as much in market is because *they don't put as much money in!*

The reasons they don't put as much money in may stem from cultural upbringing or discrimination. I know of one family that received $25,000 in an insurance settlement. They didn't trust the bank, so for years they left the money in a shoebox under the bed. They had lived on a cash basis from week to week and month to month, and simply had no experience with banks or investing, so they simply did not know how to invest it, and didn't trust anyone. The point I want to make here is that the *lack of access* to knowledge is discriminatory! The information in this book is designed to help fight that kind of discrimination.

All other factors being equal, those having access to the information in *The Millionaire Machine* will have greater access to financial independence than those not having access to this information. I wrote this book for anyone who wants greater personal financial control and stability, and a better future with better planning. If, however, black women do not receive this information, they cannot use it. I would like to see everyone have equal access to the information in *The Millionaire Machine,* and to have it as soon as possible. When you read the book: You will know how important TIME is!

The truth is that most people who have a job can become millionaires–if they want to be! You can too! All you have to do is know how and follow the plan!

Introduction

Author: "OK. What do you want?"

Reader: " I want a MILLION DOLLARS."

Author: "Everyone wants a million dollars. That is most likely
possible? Now, what do you have to offer?"

Reader: "What do you mean what do I have to offer? I want
a million dollars."

Author: "I'm not going to give you a million dollars. I will tell
you how to make a million dollars, but you have to
put something into it."

Reader: "I don't have a million dollars. What do I have to put in
to this thing?"

Author: "Money. Not a whole lot; but you must have a job or some
source of income."

Reader: "Yea, I've got a job. But I don't make enough money to
become a millionaire."

Author: "You can become a millionaire on $2,000 a year! You don't
believe it right now, but I will show you how to do it. You will
also need a "good" interest rate–say 16%–and you will also
need some time."

Reader: "I can do the $2,000 a year. Now, how hard is it to find
that 16% interest? And, how long will it take to reach
a million dollars at 16%?"

Author: "That 16% interest isn't hard to find. It's *2% less* than the
the stock market average of 18% for the last 20 years.
Sixteen percent and $2,000 a year will get you to a million
dollars in *29 years*."

Reader: "I want the million dollars now. I don't want to wait 29
years. Can we do anything to get it faster!"

Author: "I think I've got your attention! A few minutes ago you didn't even believe you could make a million. Now, you can't make it fast enough. Sure, we can get there faster. Just increase the amount of money, the interest rate, or both. In fact my original title for this book was; "The weight of time, and *how* to *buy* it!"

Reader: "What is the best I can do? If I really can become a millionaire; I want to be one as soon as I can! Can I really believe you?"

Author: "If you can put away $10,000 a year at 20% interest or better, you're looking at a million in less than 15 years. It's entirely your decision whether getting that million is worth the sacrifices."

Reader: "What do I have to sacrifice for the million? Are you the devil and I have to sell you my soul or something?"

Author: "Just lifestyle changes. You must really set aside the money and invest it at these interest rates. You really have to do it. Just thinking about it won't make it happen! So, when do you want your million?"

Reader: "Someday, I really can have a million dollars? And how soon I get the million dollars depends on how much I can invest; and, the interest rate at which I invest?"

Author: " That is exactly what the equation says: *Money* times *Interest* times *TIME* = $1,000,000.00 "

The Millionaire Machine

The Price of Time

You really do want to be a millionaire someday. Make that "as soon as possible! Now, let's look and see what we have to work with. You get up and go to work, get paid, pay the bills, spend some money, and hopefully have some money left over. It is this money you have left over that we must work with.

Let's jump ahead and say you have put aside $2,000 per year for 29 years @ 16% average return on your savings. You now have $1,058,622. Of this amount, you contributed $58,000. ($2,000 per year for 29 years.) The other $1,000,622 comes from interest. You put up only 5.479% of the money, and interest accounts for 94.521%. That is not a bad deal. For every dollar you put in you get back at least seventeen dollars. The only "problem" is it takes 29 years to generate this result @ $2,000 per year and 16% average interest.

What we must do is to take those dollars you have left over after paying bills, and multiply them, several times, in the shortest possible time period. We must find ways to "buy time" to make it possible for you to become wealthy– hopefully in less than 29 years.

Well, let me introduce you to a couple who started putting $10,000 a year into mutual funds 15 years ago. Their funds have averaged 22%, and they now have $1,039,345. They have contributed $150,000 ($10,000 per year for 15 years.) Interest accounts for $889,345. They don't get back nearly as much per dollar invested as the guy with 2,000 a year at 16%. They get back less than six dollars for each dollar contributed–but they contributed more and get to the million dollar level in about half the time. (15 years rather than 29 years.) They have succeeded in "buying" 14 years.

	2000/yr. @16%	10,000/yr@22%	Difference
Total:	$1,058,622	$1,039,345	$19,277 less
Amt. Invest:	$ 58,000	$ 150,000	$92,000 more
Amt. Interest:	$1,000,622	$ 889,345	$111,277 less
TIME:	29 years	15 years	14 Years

The couple investing $10,000 per year at 22% hit the million mark 14 YEARS SOONER. The price to do this is to invest $92,000 more and to get $111,277 less interest. The person(s) investing $2,000 a year at 16% must spend 14 more years to make it to the million level. How much are those 14 years worth?

The point I want to make here is the relationship between how much is invested, the average rate of interest, and the amount of TIME that it is invested for. If you want a million dollars, you can BUY it for $2,000/yr. @16% (29 YEARS) or $10,000/yr. @ 22% (15 YEARS); or, at several other possibilities.

The purpose of this book is to explore these possibilities on a mathematical basis–that is the way you get to the million(s).

I see descriptive books that tell how much millionaires pay for shoes or cars, or how much their houses are worth. But paying that much (or that little) for your shoes or your car will not make you a millionaire. By the way, most millionaires just barely made it. Most are worth less than $1,250,000 and have a house worth $300,000 to $450,000. The house makes up 25 to 40% of their wealth. Typical incomes are over $200,000 per year. Sure, the high incomes and big houses help make them millionaires; but the big houses and high incomes are not necessary to become millionaires.

Other books tell you how to invest in very minute detail. Good, but do you need to know all the technical jargon in order to make good investments and to make money? I prefer to tell you how much you need to invest, for how long, and at what interest rates to reach your goals of financial security. Others can tell you how much you should pay for food, clothing, rent, mortgage, and other expenses. Or how much millionaires pay for socks and underwear. It makes for good reading–but does it really tell you how to become a millionaire?

You no longer have to win a lottery jackpot or win a million on a TV game show. You can give yourself a million, and the outcome has much greater certainty! Here you learn how to use Money, Interest, and TIME to achieve your financial goals.

More Conversation with the Author.

Reader: "Do I really need to invest for my future? I don't really want much–just enough to pay the rent, buy food, have decent transportation, and some left over for entertainment. The Social Security Administration just sent me a statement telling me how much I will collect in Social Security when I retire–so they are looking after me. I may not have any money to invest; and besides, I can save a few dollars on your book if I wait till it comes out in paperback."

Author: "Actually that statement is telling you how *little* you will receive from Social Security! They want to give you knowledge and time to supplement it with other savings and investments. If you don't do something for yourself, that statement amount is all you will get! Social Security was never intended to be a "retirement fund." Just a fund to help supplement other pension funds. Today, many employers have stopped contributions to pension funds. If you want anything, you must make the contributions. If you contribute nothing, nothing is what you will get!

There are no plans for a paperback version yet. If there is a paperback version, it could take a few years. Waiting for it could cost you one or two doubling periods. That is too expensive to wait for! Loss of those doubling periods could easily cost $500,000 or more. What I try to sell you is the knowledge of how to make more money, and the importance of TIME to do it!"

There are a lot of books that promise to be "blueprints" and "maps" on how to become a millionaire. I believe this 'concept' is designed to confuse the average person. As an engineer, I know that most people can't read a blueprint, and many can't read a map either! These books imply that you need a blueprint to "build" a million; or need a map to "find" a million. I don't believe you build or find financial security; you plan it and then you achieve it.

A Note about Fraud

What happens when someone writes a book that really does allow ordinary people the opportunity to become millionaires, or at least to become financially independent? Will the book be treated as just another one of those books supposedly telling you how to make money–even millions–but in reality, all it does is move money from your pocket to the author's pocket? If something is promised–and that promise is not delivered upon–it is fraud–and it is illegal! If you find something that fits that description, call the Better Business Bureau and/or the FBI. You will find your local FBI number listed inside the front cover of your Yellow Pages.

There are hefty fines and jail sentences for selling fraudulent products across state lines. Personally I'd like to see these penalties increased, since every book I have ever read that told me "how to make large sums of money" fell well short of its promises.

Many of these books try to sell you something; and–if you buy it–you supposedly will make a lot of money. Sometimes a company will use this approach in an effort to sell their stock, insurance policies, or other financial instruments. There are some that tell you, "If you had put $10,000 in this fund 10 years ago, you would have $20,000 now." No false advertising here; it is very true. The value of the fund doubled in ten years. I consider that a lousy investment. We want our money to double faster than that. How about every five years?

	Doubles in 10 yrs	Doubles in 5 yrs
Beginning Investment:	$10,000	$10,000
After 5 years:	$15,000	$20,000
After 10 years:	$20,000	$40,000

If you are willing to accept "doubling your money" every 10 years, please put this book back on the shelf and forget about it! MY ACCEPTABLE INTEREST RATES DON'T GO THAT LOW! I want you to put money into funds that will get you to Financial Independence, and maybe to "millionaire." Hard to do? Let's take just the standard $2,000 per year IRA deduction. Invest it at 16% Interest each year, and in 29 years YOU HAVE YOUR MILLION!

Please look at the chart on the following page. It shows the result of doubling an investment of $2,000 or $4,000 per year.

Years	$2,000/yr	$4,000/yr
30	$1,230,322	$2,460,644
29	**1,058,622**	2,117,244
28	910,605	1,821,210
27	783,004	1,566,008
26	673,003	1,346,006
25	**578,175**	**1,156,350**
24	496,427	992,854
23	425,954	851,908
22	365,201	730,402
21	312,829	625,658
20	267,680	**535,360**

At 16% annual interest–and just $2,000 per year–we have our million in 29 years. In fact, we get to the half-million level before 25 years! Please notice that if we can invest $4,000 per year at 16% we can reach a million in 25 years, and a half million in 20 years. Notice that our investment here DOUBLES about every 5th year. Do you still think that fund above that doubles every 10 years is a good deal?

The reality is that most of you will not become millionaires. You will get off the wagon before you reach the million level–say, at the $500,000 to $700,000 level. That is OK with me, if you are satisfied with that result.

If you put more money into investments at higher rates you can make it to your goals even sooner. So, if you don't have anything better to do, you may as well become a millionaire! If you do have something better to do please write to me and tell me about it! I have a great sense of humor and like to laugh. (PO Box 1031, Dearborn Hts, MI 48127, or E-mail to wla54@hotmail.com.)

How to do the Math!

In a previous book I had a reader write in and thank me for explaining the subject in a clear and easy to understand manner–except that I used mathematics! Well, the problem had a mathematical solution; it could not be solved by anything other than mathematics. I sometimes respond that: "If a recipe for meatloaf would solve the problem, I would use it. However it doesn't; therefore I must use mathematics."

To do your own calculations you will require a scientific calculator with only one additional function: Y to the X power (or Y^X.) This will do all the compound interest calculation you will need in this book.

Example: If we put $100 into an account and get 1% interest each month, what do we get in one year? Some will jump to say 12%. But that is wrong; we will get a little more. Here is the equation: pick up the scientific calculator and do this yourself:

1.01 Y^X12 = 1.1268. The 1. means that we maintain the existing balance. The .01 is the interest rate that we receive. The 12 is the number of periods during which we get interest. If we multiply $100 times the above equation we will get $112.683. That is the total amount we will have after 12 months.

If we want to invest $1,000 @ 12% for 10 years, the equation looks like this:

$1,000 x (1.12$Y^X$10)= $3,105.848

(.12 is the interest rate. 10 is the number of years.)

How does that compare with 1% each month for 10 years?

$1,000 x (1.01$Y^X$120) = $3,300.386

(.01 is the interest rate. 120 is the number of months.)

Interesting. COMPOUNDING the INTEREST each month gets an additional $194.54 in interest at the end of the ten years compared to compounding the interest each year. The "magic" of Compounding is extremely important. Pay attention to compounding in every investment you make.

Note that simple 12% interest each year would earn $120 per year times 10 years = $1,200 in interest *plus* the original balance of $1,000 = $2,200.00. Notice the much better result of compound interest over simple interest. Most of us would rather have the compound interest above.

All of the tables in the back of this book are calculated this way: The calculations are done for each year, and then added to the totals for the previous year for the cumulative tables. The non-cumulative tables are just for that number of years; no interest from previous years is added. With the above information you will be able to do any compound interest calculation. Less than 1% of the population of the United States can calculate compound interest. The rest of the world is not much better. That knowledge can help you become a millionaire.

Retirement Math

Most of you will not wait for the million. You will "bail out" around $400,000 to $600,000 when you find that you can have a lot of fun on the interest on these amounts. Ten percent interest on those amounts gives you $40,000 to 60,000 before taxes. Fifteen percent gives you $60,000 to $90,000 per year before taxes. Both of these are well above the national income averages.

How much do you need to retire? Most analysts suggest that you should aim for about 80% of your income before you retire. Figure out how much you will need before taxes. Say $50,000/yr. How much in investments do we need to generate that amount at, say, 12.5% interest? Here it is:

$50,000 times (1/.125) = $400,000

You can also use $50,000 times (.125) times 1/x = $400,000

Check: $400,000 times .125 = $50,000

Say you want $4,000 per month in income before taxes. How much in investments do you need to generate this at 10% annual interest?

Hint: 10% per year = 10/12 months = .00833 interest per month.

So: $4,000/month times (.00833) times (1/x) = $480,192.07

Check: $480,192.07 times (.00833) = $3,999.9999

The Weight of Money

One of the themes of this book is to "measure" the importance of the three variables: Money, Interest, and TIME.

The following table shows us the results of investing a fixed amount of money for a fixed time period–in this case a year–at a fixed interest rate. Here we increase the amount of money to be invested by $2000 at each interval. What the chart shows is that for each $2,000 we invest, we get $2,160 back, the difference being the result the 8% interest we earned.

M (Money) increases by $2,000 on each line. I (Interest) = 8% and T (Time) = 1 year

Amount Invested	Return @ 8%	Difference
$ 20,000	$ 21,600	$ 2,160
$ 18,000	$ 19,440	$ 2,160
$ 16,000	$ 17,280	$ 2,160
$ 14,000	$ 15,120	$ 2,160
$ 12,000	$ 12,960	$ 2,160
$ 10,000	$ 10,800	$ 2,160
$ 8,000	$ 8,640	$ 2,160
$ 6,000	$ 6,480	$ 2,160
$ 4,000	$ 4,320	$ 2,160
$ 2.000	$ 2,160	

As the money invested increases at a $2,000 increment, the return increases at a rate of $2,160. Note that this is constant; it is always the same. It does not increase or decrease. Compare this result to the result from changes in Interest and changes in Time.

The Weight of Interest

Here we keep the amount of Money constant, vary the rate of Interest by 2%, and keep the Time interval constant at 1 year. We start at 8% interest and go all the way up to 26%–exactly the same as our tables in the back of the book.

M= $2,000, I increases by 2% on successive examples, T = 1 year.

Amount Invested	Interest Rate	1-yr Return	Difference
$ 2,000	26%	$ 2,520	$40
$ 2,000	24%	$ 2,480	$40
$ 2,000	22%	$ 2,440	$40
$ 2,000	20%	$ 2,400	$40
$ 2,000	18%	$ 2,360	$40
$ 2,000	16%	$ 2,320	$40
$ 2,000	14%	$ 2,280	$40
$ 2,000	12%	$ 2,240	$40
$ 2,000	10%	$ 2,200	$40
$ 2,000	8%	$ 2,160	----

Note that as our interest rate increases by 2%, our return increases by $40. Nowhere does this "accelerate" and give us a larger return. Of course, we would rather get the $2,520 return at 26% than the $2,160 return at 8%.

The Weight of TIME

Here we keep the amount of Money constant, keep the rate of Interest at 8%, and vary the Time interval by 1 year. We calculate the results for 1 through 10 years. Note that no additional investment is made beyond our original $2,000.

M= $2,000   I = 8%   T increases by 1 year.

Amount Invested	Years	Return	Difference
$ 2,000	10	$ 4,312.85	$ 319.85
$ 2,000	9	$ 3,998.00	$ 296.12
$ 2,000	8	$ 3,761.86	$ 274.21
$ 2,000	7	$ 3,427.65	$ 253.90
$ 2,000	6	$ 3,173.75	$ 235.10
$ 2,000	5	$ 2,938.65	$ 217.67
$ 2,000	4	$ 2,720.98	$ 201.56
$ 2,000	3	$ 2,519.42	$ 186.62
$ 2,000	2	$ 2,352.80	$ 172.90
$ 2,000	1	$ 2,160.00	----

Note that in this example we get a larger amount of return each successive year. This is the advantage of TIME! In the other examples we got back exactly the same amount of increase per each additional unit of input. Here we get back even more per each additional unit of time. Again we are looking at the "magic" of compounding.

A major example of the importance of time is the following: Here we have three individuals with retirement as their goal. Let's conisider a 33 year time period. Each investment is for $2,000 per year and all interest rates are the same—in this example 12% per year. Mr. A puts in $2,000 per year for only the first 10 years; then leaves the money to collect 12% interest for each successive year—but he puts no additional money into the account!

Mr. B. doesn't put any money away for the first 10 years; then he puts $2,000 per year in for then next 10 years, and stops. Mr. B then puts no more money into the account; but continues to get 12% interest on it each year.

Mr. C. puts no money away for the first 10 years. Then he invests $2,000 per year in every year until he reaches age 62.

See how important those first ten years are! Mr. B will never catch Mr. A. He will always be behind him; and with each passing year the gap will widen. Mr. C does a little bit better; but the gap still widens between him and Mr. A. Mr. C will not catch up with Mr. A in this lifetime. (And that is all the time we have to work with!)

$2,000/yr.	12% Interest			
Year	**Age**	**Mr. A**	**Mr. B**	**Mr. C**
33	62	$532,731	$171,525	$226,593
32	61	475,653	153,147	202,392
31	60	424,690	136,738	180,784
30	59	379,187	122,088	159,177
29	58	338,560	109,007	139,884
28	57	302,286	97,328	122,659
27	56	269,898	86,900	107,279
26	55	240,980	77,589	93,547
25	54	215,161	69,276	81,286
24	53	192,108	61,853	71,512
23	52	171,525	55,226	62,785
22	51	153,147	49,309	54,058
21	50	136,738	44,026	46,266
20	49	122,088	39,309	39,309
19	48	109,007	33,097	33,097
18	47	97,328	27,551	27,551
17	46	86,900	22,599	22,599
16	45	77,589	18,178	18,178
15	44	69,276	14,230	14,230
14	43	61,853	10,705	10,705
13	42	55,226	7,558	7,558
12	41	49,309	4,748	4,748
11	40	44,026	2,240	2,240
10	39	39,309	0	,0
9	38	33,097	0	0
8	37	27,551	0	0
7	36	22,599	0	0
6	35	18,178	0	0
5	34	14,230	0	0
4	33	10,705	0	0
3	32	7,558	0	0
2	31	4,748	0	0
1	30	2,240	0	0

If the amount of money invested is more or the interest rate is higher; the differences between the three investing styles will be greater. See the table on the next page for the same kind of comparison but with a 16% interest rate.

$2,000/yr.	16% interest			
Year	AGE	Mr. A	Mr. B	Mr. C
33	62	$1,502,584	$340,611	$425,954
32	61	1,295,331	293,630	365,201
31	60	1,116,664	253,129	312,829
30	59	962,642	218,215	267,680
29	58	839,863	188,116	228,758
28	57	715,399	162,169	195,205
27	56	616,724	139,801	166,280
26	55	531,658	120,518	141,345
25	54	458,326	103,895	119,849
24	53	395,109	89,564	101,318
23	52	340,611	77,210	85,343
22	51	293,630	66,561	71,571
21	50	253,129	57,380	59,699
20	49	218,215	49,465	49,465
19	48	188,116	40,642	40,642
18	47	162,169	33,037	33,037
17	46	139,801	26,480	26,480
16	45	120,518	20,827	20,827
15	44	103,895	15,954	15,954
14	43	89,564	11,754	11,754
13	42	77,210	8,132	8,132
12	41	66,561	5,011	5,011
11	40	57,380	2,320	2,320
10	39	49,465	0	,0
9	38	40,642	0	0
8	37	33,037	0	0
7	36	26,480	0	0
6	35	20,827	0	0
5	34	15,954	0	0
4	33	11,754	0	0
3	32	8,132	0	0
2	31	5,011	0	0
1	30	2,320	0	0

Notice how much wider the gap increases in this table with a 16% interest rate. Note that Mr. A and Mr. B contributed the same amount to the accounts ($20,000.00) and that Mr. C. gave even more ($66,000.00). Neither Mr. B. nor Mr. C. can catch up with Mr. A. That 10-year head start is just too much. The real question of course is "Which of these investors do you want to be!"

What this means is that TIME is the variable with the potential to give back the largest amount. We must make the most efficient use of TIME because it is our most important variable! We must invest as soon as possible. If *You* waste TIME, TIME will find a way to waste *you!*

Here are some other important aspects of TIME for anyone reading this book:

Your age at the time you read *The Millionaire Machine* may be the most important aspect of TIME! Your age will determine at what age you can become a millionaire, and consequently, how many years you will enjoy the benefits. For example, if you are thirty, you can become a millionaire somewhere between ages 45 and 55. However, if you are 40, you most likely will achieve that goal between 55 and 65. Your age also has a great effect on your earning potential for the rest of your life. The person reading the book at age 30 will probably have about 10 years more earning potential than the one who is 40. Check the tables and see how much difference there is in a 10 year period!

The person above who reads *The Millionaire Machine* at 30 and becomes a millionaire at age 45 has 10 more years to "make money" compared to the person who reads it at 40 and becomes a millionaire at 55. In other words the 45 year old millionaire will probably live longer than the 55 year old millionaire. He will most likely have more years to enjoy an enriched lifestyle! A major benefit of TIME!

The Difference between Saving and Investing.

The difference between saving and investing is very clear to me. Money in "savings" is there for specific purposes: to pay future bills, to take a vacation, to pay upcoming taxes, to buy a piano, or for other such specific goals. I don't really plan on this money playing any part in my retirement, or having a long-tern effect on my financial future. I expect that financial growth to come from funds other than "savings".

I would therefore define "savings" as money put aside to cover future expenses, but not expected to make a significant contribution to retirement funds. As for interest, I would accept less than 10% for a savings fund, but that goal *is entirely too low for a retirement fund.* The primary function of "savings" is to be there; that is, to exist when those bills must be paid, to cover those expenses when they come due. Without the existence of such a fund, expenses would be paid from interest-bearing retirement funds, thereby eroding future earning potential!

One day, Najwa, the assistant manager at my bank, invited me to come by and to bring all my IRA funds. She had assured me that they could give me better interest rates. Well, with nothing to lose, I wanted to take Najwa up on her offer. But the bank could not equal the interest rates of any of my IRA funds. Then I noticed that I had a small IRA fund that I had started at the bank many years before and had not rolled-over. The fund paid a fixed annual interest rate. When it was started years ago the rate was at about 18%, but over the years had dropped to 5% annual interest.

It was time to move this IRA money into something paying much more interest.

Najwa did point out to me that the bank's stock was earning about 22% annual interest, and that I should buy some. I looked through my portfolios and sure enough, one of my IRA funds already had a large block of the bank's stock. I asked her if she had any of the bank's stock in her 401(k) plans. She didn't. I then showed her how fast money could accumulate at 22%:

Years	$2,000/yr	$4,000/yr	$6,000/yr	$8,000/yr	$10,000/yr
20	**$580,693**	**$1,161,386**	$1,742,079	$2,322,772	$2,903,465
19	473,978	947,956	1,421,934	1,895,912	2,369,890
18	386,507	773,014	**1,159,521**	1,546,028	1,932,535
17	314,809	629,618	944,427	1,259,236	1,574,045
16	256,040	**512,080**	768,120	**1,024,160**	1,280,200
15	207,869	415,738	623,607	831,476	**1,039,345**
14	168,384	336,768	**505,152**	673,536	841,920
13	136,020	272,040	408,060	**544,080**	680,100
12	109,491	218,982	328,473	437,964	**547,455**
11	87,747	175,494	263,241	350,988	438,735
10	69,924	139,848	209,772	279,696	349,620
9	53,314	106,628	159,942	213,256	266,570
8	43,340	86,680	130,020	173,360	216,700
7	33,524	67,048	100,572	134,096	167,620
6	25,479	50,958	76,437	101,916	127,395
5	18,884	37,768	56,652	75,536	94,420
4	13,479	26,958	40,437	53,916	67,395
3	9,048	18,096	27,144	36,192	45,240
2	5,416	10,832	16,248	21,664	27,080
1	2,440	4,880	7,320	9,760	12,200

WOW! Look at that! With an investment of $10,000 per year--you can have over half a million dollars in 12 years! And a **MILLION** dollars *in 15 years!*

If I put my money in the bank, I'll get 6% or less in interest. (My interest tables only go as low as 6%!) If I buy the bank's stock, I get about 22%. If: I put my money in the bank, my money and I are working to make money for the bank! However, if I buy the bank's stock, it is working to make money for me! The latter sounds so much better!

Najwa had been at the bank for 8 years and had not joined the 401(k) retirement plan. Lets look at where her plan would be had she set aside $4,000 per year.

Year	Invest-ment	begin balance	% interest	Balance	Bal @ 16.625%
8	$ 4000	$ 52,777	22%	$ 69,267	$ 66,827
7	$ 4000	$ 40,727	18%	$ 52,777	$ 53,485
6	$ 4000	$ 31,726	14%	$ 40,727	$ 42,009
5	$ 4000	$ 23,350	16%	$ 31,726	$ 32,137
4	$ 4000	$ 16,305	15%	$ 23,350	$ 23,644
3	$ 4000	$ 9,936	17%	$ 16,305	$ 16,339
2	$ 4000	$ 4,640	15%	$ 9,936	$ 10,055
1	$ 4000	$ 4,000	16%	$ 4,640	$ 4,650

Note: The last column is the straight line balance of 16.625% per year. Both columns reflect an "average" balance of 16.625% per year. There is variance depending on how much is earned each year! The straight line interest of 15.625% each year is better until the 22% payout in year 8. Please note that the cumulative tables in back of book are based on this "straight-line" method because I don't know where and how much variance to add.

Either way, Najwa would have invested $32,000 and gotten back at least $69,267 in just eight years. This would be just her "nest-egg" for the present time. Let's say Najwa adds nothing to this 401(k). What could she expect in the future?

$ 145,484.37 in five years @ 16% average interest,
$ 305,566.87 in ten years @ 16% average interest, or
$ 641,794.83 in fifteen years @ 16% average interest.

At this 16% average interest rate, Najwa can expect her money to double every 4.7 years. ($1.16 Y^X \underline{4.7} = 2.00887$.)

Of course this is a "what-if" scenario. Najwa has worked at the bank eight years but as yet has not invested anything at all in her 401(k) plan. She cannot reach any of these levels until she begins to invest at year one. If she had started investing the $ 4,000 per year as soon as she was eligible, these numbers would be in real dollars!

"Lifestyles"

To become a millionaire, some change in lifestyle may be required. One person explained that it is not possible for him to become a millionaire because: " I have about $20,000 in credit card debt. I spend all my money trying to get out of that debt! I just can't afford to become a millionaire right now!" I have just a little bit of trouble following that logic.

If this person can change the conditions to meet the "millionaire equation" he can become a millionaire. He believes that he does not have the necessary money to become a millionaire. It is up to him to find a way to meet those requirements. Set up a plan to pay off that debt; or start the investments and pay off the debt over a longer time period.

Another example I get is: "I put the money in mutual funds like you suggest, but my funds only earned 8% interest." Or, "I put my money in bank CDs and the interest was only 5.5%." If you under-invest with a low interest rate, you will not get the desired rate of return. You will not get as much money as I indicate you should.

Another example is someone who transfers money into another fund before interest is paid, or before the desired time frame. "I put this money into this 20% fund for six months; but I only got 10% interest, so I moved it to another fund." If it had been left in for a full year, it would have gotten the full 20%.

The "Millionaire Equation" must be followed in all three elements: **Money, Interest,** and **TIME.** If you get the most from these three elements, you will achieve the desired results. Omit or fall short on any one of them and you will be short of your objectives!

If changes in your lifestyle are necessary to fulfill the equation, you *must* make them. Someone said to me, "I can't afford to invest that much. I have to keep up my CD collection. I have all Jackson's and several others!" This person's priorities are to advance the financial future of millionaire rock stars or sports stars before "advancing" his own financial future.

The "Jacksons":

Jackson	Occupation	Known For
Reggie Jackson	Baseball player	Genius-Smartest Jackson?
Bo Jackson	Baseball/Football player	Did Know Diddly?
Michael Jackson	Rock star	Makes most money?
Jesse Jackson	Politician	Hostage releases?

I haven't included all the Jacksons, just a few. All of them would take several books. I'm not going to tell you not to spend money on any of the Jacksons, but since they are all rather well-off financially, I am going to tell you to take care of *your* necessary investments first. Then, you can spend *dis-cretionary money* on the Jacksons. *You are your most important investment. Pay yourself first!*

   Taking care of your future, whether becoming a millionaire or financially independent is your first priority!

   In contrast to those who look at reasons "why they can't follow the "millionaire equation," there are some who take part-time jobs so they can invest more.

   Example: One person took a part-time job so he could afford to add $3,000 more per year to his retirement plan. See what this $3,000 per year returns in years 11 through 20:

Year	Invest	Total Return @ 12.5%	
20	$3,000	$31,635	
19	$3,000	$28,120	
18	$3,000	$24,995	
17	$3,000	$22,218	
16	$3,000	$19,749	
			$126,717
15	$3,000	$17,555	
14	$3,000	$15,604	
13	$3,000	$13,870	
12	$3,000	$12,329	
11	$3,000	$10,959	
			$70,317

   The total revenues for these 10 years–made possible by a part-time job paying just $3,000 per year are $197,034. ($126,717 + $70,317)

   If you want to become a millionaire or to gain financial independence; you must establish that goal as a major priority. Some examples of lifestyle changes are:

   A) A former sports fan who no longer goes to any sports games.

   "They went on strike, and I haven't gone back. I'm not going to pay a lot of money to watch a bunch of millionaires play a kids' game–unless it's free. At least not until I have a million of my own!" He does watch the games on TV if he has nothing better to do. His attitude is: "I deserve my money more than they do!"

   B) A rock fan who no longer goes to concerts–except when business associates treat. He has sold most of his CD collection and put the proceeds into no-load mutual funds. He even called me to ask where he could find no-load mutual funds. (Bank did not offer a good rate.) I told him to look for their (800) numbers in *The Wall Street Journal* or in other financial magazines.

C) A rather wealthy person I know recently returned from vacation and found several bills waiting. Although he paid them immediately, one credit card bill was late. The next month he received a $29 late fee. He cut up the card and sent it in with a check for the $29. The next month he got a bill for 45 cents in interest on the $29. He sent a check for one dollar: "They got me for $29.45. They will get no more business from me!"

D) Another person doesn't like advertisements: "I make it a point not to buy any product I see advertised. Hey, I know who pays the costs to advertise those products. I do in the form of higher prices! And I don't like it. I try to boycott those who try to get me with inferior products or higher costs, including advertising. I also boycott the sports and movie stars they hire to promote products. I don't watch their sports or movies. I guess I save about $3,000 to $4,000 every year. That goes directly into investments. Better that I get the money than they do–at least until I have my Million!"

You never had any idea that you could become a millionaire. What "life style" changes will you make when you suddenly change you goals? How much priority does becoming a millionaire have for you?

E) Five years ago, Ricardo moved into a new house using the $50,000 equity in his old house as a down-payment and taking a 30-year mortgage on the balance of $260,000. Ricardo's monthly payment was just over $1,800. After reading the manuscript for *The Millionaire Machine*, Ricardo is re-thinking his "dream-house." In three years, Ricardo's youngest child graduates from high school. At that time Recardo plans on selling his "dream-house."

"I'll use the equity for payment on a new, smaller house and start an investment fund of $10,000 to $12,000 per year. In 22 years I should have nearly a million dollars. Will my present $260,000 "dream-house" be worth that much?"

Why Mutual Funds? How to Read

Why Mutual Funds? I choose mutual funds because they are, by their very nature already diversified. They are made up of a number of stocks, so the risk is spread over several companies and several categories of investments. If you place all your money in one company's stock, and problems develop in that company, you may lose a large portion of your investment. However, with mutual funds, if one company's stock drops in value, the rest of the fund's holdings would be unaffected.

Another reason I like mutual funds is that some come in a "no-load" variety. That means you pay no sales fee when you buy them, and you pay no sales fee when you sell them or transfer them. After expenses of operating the fund, all the earnings go to the fund's shareholders. You don't have to share interest with anyone. That makes them grow even faster. Don't worry; the operators get paid. They take out expenses before any dividends or interest is paid.

How to keep track of your funds: Almost every daily newspaper in the United States lists the net asset values of many mutual funds. They will usually be near the pages for the varous stock exchange listings. My daily newspaper lists the value of the mutual fund at the last close. How much it was up or down, and one of the following:

A)	What the fund earned for the last 13 weeks.	Monday
B)	What the fund earned for the last 26 weeks.	Tuesday
C)	What the fund earned for the last year.	Wednesday
D)	What the fund earned for the last 3 years.	Thursday
E)	What the fund earned for the last 5 years.	Friday
F)	The expense ratio of the fund.	Saturday

If you read this newspaper for the entire week, you have a history of how well the fund has performed from the last 13 weeks to the last 5 years. Sometimes newspapers will list all of these on the same day:

Mutual Fund	St at us	Close	Diff	13wks	6 Mo	1 Yr	3 Yrs	5 Yrs	10Yrs
ABC	n	18.10	-.16	12.5	5.4	3.7	9.1	8.2	9.2
DEF	n	15.34	-.21	-4.2	3.4	6.8	7.1	6.9	7.1
GHI	n	92.16	+.42	-1.3	8.6	12.6	15.8	13.2	13.8
JKL	n	47.31	+.27	3.7	9.2	15.8	17.4	19.2	*24.6*
MNO	n	4.02	-----	9.2	10.6	11.0	9.9	*10.2*	10.1
PQR	n	27.21	+.04	17.4	13.9	14.6	16.2	13.5	11.8
STU	n	13.95	-.03	-2.0	7.0	14.1	13.8	12.5	11.2
VWX	n	24.76	-.02	4.3	16.2	18.4	22.4	19.2	18.4
YZA	n	58.05	+.15	13.4	21.2	*27.1*	22.1	20.4	19.6

Please note that those rates listed for more than one year are the average rates per year–not the total amount of interest that has been paid. Example: Fund JKL has gained 24.6% for each of the last 10 years. That is a total return of **901%.** ($1.\underline{246}\ Y^X 10 = 9.01$). Fund MNO has averaged a gain of 10.2% for each of the last 5 years. That is a total payback of **162.5%.** ($1.102\ Y^X$ power $5 = 1.625$). Fund YZA gained 27.1% in the last year. But it has returned an average of 19.6% for each of the last 10 years. That 19.6% for 10 years is a total return of **5.988 times.**

In the "status" column, "n" means no-load funds. This example does not represent a very volatile day for the market. Notice that none of the funds changed more than one percent for the day. (+0.5% to -0.8%) The "Diff" column is sometimes called "Change." Sometimes, instead of indicating how much the value went up or down; it will just list "last." If "last" were listed for ABC in the table above it would show "18.26." It is now listed at 18.10; therefore it is down .16 per the chart above. If, "last" is mentioned instead of change you must sub-tract one from the other to determine how much the value has changed.

We have 10 years of history for each of the funds listed above. Three funds (DEF, GHI, and STU) are down for the past 13 weeks. However for the last 6 months and last year all are up. These are within the ranges of normal fluctuations and all may again be up in the next quarter (13 weeks.)
All are higher for 1 year than for 6 months. These may be cyclic funds that make most of their income in December and are therefore higher at that time of the year. The market typically goes up early in the year with purchases of IRAs be-fore income tax filing, and usually goes up near end of year, the time most funds pay out capital gains distributions. Summer usually lags. Not much happens.

Suppose we set our goal to make 20%. Which of the above funds look promising?

Mutual Fund	Status	Close	Diff	13 wks	6 Mo	1 Yr	3 Yrs	5 Yrs	10 Yrs
		Price							
JKL	n	47.31	+.27	3.7	9.2	15.8	17.4	19.2	**24.6**
VWX	n	24.76	-.02	4.3	16.2	18.4	**22.4**	19.2	18.4
YZA	n	58.05	+.15	13.4	**21.2**	27.1	22.1	20.4	19.6

We see only these three funds that have been increased by over 20% at any time over the last 5 years. PQR is up 17.4% for the last 13 weeks. However, it has not been at 20% at any time. It must go above past performances to get to our 20% goal. Let's look elsewhere. JKL has gained 24.6% annually over the last 10 years–except for last year, when the gain was only 15.8%.

VWX meets our 20% goal for the last 3 years (22.4%.) However, it is short for the 10-year average, and also has fallen off for the past year (18.4% for 1 year; and only 16.2% for last 6 months.)

Probably the best bet for a 20% or better return is YZA. It is very close for a 10-year average (19.6%). And for all reported periods in the last 5 years it has been over 20%. Looking at the last 13 weeks (13.4%,) I don't believe it will gain at this rate for a whole year. That would be more than 52% (4 times 13%.) However, a return of 20 to 26% is very probable; in fact it may do even better. Let's put our money in the fund most likely to get our 20%–or more!

Notes on the Case Studies

I have used case studies of real situations to teach some principles of investing. I am hopeful that you can learn from others–especially from their mistakes. You will probably not live long enough to make all the mistakes yourself. Therefore it will be necessary to learn from others. Here are the ideas I had in mind when I wrote these:

Case 1:   Don't reinvest at lower interest rates.

Case 2:   Have a Plan, and use TIME to your best advantage.

Case 3:   Defer taxes where possible. The government is
            not a good "partner".

Case 4:   A million and financial independence are possible.
            Start as soon–and with as much–as possible.

Case 5:   "No Goals" "No Plans" There is always tomorrow.
            But what happens when "tomorrow" arrives?

Case 6:   Learn to see "long-term," not just "short-term".

Case 7:   50 is late to start. But is not too late!

Case 8:   Where are we? What time is it? Too late for early
            retirement.

Case 9:   On Track. Early retirement, or financial
            independence.

Case 10:   Company didn't want to pay pensions. Created
            financial opportunities.

Case 11:   No Goals, Plans, or Directions. Settle for much
            less than what is possible.

Case 12:   Adjusted lifestyle to spending $240,000 per year, and saving
nothing. Some adjustment will be necessary soon.

Case 13:   A Millionaire!

Case 14:   The "goal" of this business is not to generate profits for owners. It is to produce jobs for relatives.

Case 15:   This is your story. What will happen?

Another reason I used a case-study approach is that I wanted to avoid writing a textbook. I could have made it a textbook and made it about 400 pages of economic terms, stock-market jargon, e-net, on-line trading, etc. But there are already enough of these, and few of them work on long term plans and goals.

The Harvard Business School was the first to use a case-study approach, and almost all the best business schools now use these methods. Rumor is that a great number of Harvard graduates become millionaires! I wonder how many were millionaires before Harvard? Case studies represent real-life circumstances, problems, and solutions. Case studies invoke a sense of participation on the part of the reader. If case studies are good enough for Harvard, I guess they are OK for my readers. I want you to participate in something that is realistic and life-like, not a textbook. Life imitates life, not textbooks.

Case One: Airline Worker

Twenty-four years ago, a neighbor asked to borrow $200. She had received a job offer with a new little airline in a nearby city, and needed the money to move. She could have saved the money, but she wanted to move and start working right away. I lent her the money, and she sent a check paying it back the next month. A few months later I also moved to another city, and didn't hear from her till years later. I did a radio interview in the city where she lived. She heard it and called the station for my number.

Many things had happened since we had last talked. That "little" airline was no longer so "little." However, when it had been "little," cash was sometimes short, so employees were paid partially in company stock. She liked how fast the stock increased in value, and started purchasing as much company stock as she could afford. She believed it had averaged gains of just less than 15% per year, and that she had averaged buying just over $6,000 worth of stock per year.

I congratulated her, and told her she should be very close to being a millionaire by now. She asked me to do a "quick" calculation. Six years earlier she had taken out about $ 200,000 to buy rental real estate. She wanted me to tell her how much her stock fund would have been worth had she left the $200,000 in and not bought the real estate property. The real estate property had increased in value; but the increase in value and rents collected did not equal the value she would have received had that money been in company stocks.

Had she not taken the $200,000 out of her "retirement fund," she would be a millionaire–with over a $100,000 to spare!

My friend had saved up to the $600,000 level (equivalent to year 20 @ $6000/yr.) She would have, in all probability, become a millionaire in the next four years. (Year 24 on the table.) However, her penalty of $200,000 moved her back to year 17 ½ and made the million reachable in about 5 1/2 years. Notice that at this percent gain, the total value doubles approximately every 5 years. By taking out $200,000 and buying an investment that didn't equal the rate of return (14%) of her company stock, she penalized herself approximately 2 years! She won't reach a million till years later! THE WEIGHT OF TIME!

My "long lost friend" will probably become a millionaire within two more years. However, she would already be beyond the million mark if she had not taken money from the fund.

Table for 14% Cumulative Interest.

Years	$2000/yr.	$4000/yr.	$6000/yr.	$8000/yr.	$10000/yr.
30	$813,474	$1,626,948	$2,440,422	$3,253,896	$4,067,370
29	711,573	1,423,146	2,134,719	2,846,292	3,557,865
28	622,187	1,244,374	1,866,561	2,488,748	3,110,935
27	**543,778**	**1,087,556**	1,631,334	2,175,112	2,718,890
26	474,998	949,996	1,424,994	1,899,992	2,374,990
25	414,665	829,330	1,243,995	1,658,660	2,073,325
24	361,741	723,482	**1,085,223**	1,446,964	1,808,705
23	315,317	630,634	945,951	1,261,268	1,576,585
22	274,594	**549,188**	823,782	**1,098,376**	1,372,970
21	238,871	477,742	716,613	955,484	1,194,355
20	207,536	415,072	622,608	830,144	**1,037,680**
19	180,049	360,098	540,147	720,196	900,245
18	155,938	311,876	467,814	623,752	779,690
17	134,788	269,576	404,364	**539,152**	673,940
16	116,235	232,470	348,705	464,940	**581,175**

Note that the first 15 years have been deleted from the above table.

Most of you will think it was rather dumb to move $200,000 from a stock plan that was averaging 15% to real estate paying a lesser interest rate. Let's look a bit closer:

A) At the time, the stock was dropping in value. (It probably mattered little that her investment bought more shares of stock at lowered prices and that she would get a windfall when prices went back up.)

B) She saw the rental property for sale and thought: "Wouldn't it be nice to have some money coming in from rent every month!" (Remember, her stock was in a down cycle, and dropping in value.)

C) The rental property would hold its value with less fluctuation than stocks. True, it would not fluctuate in value as much as the stock, and, if enough units were rented, it would provide income each month. Rent and appreciation in value would be about 8% each year. With these three facts, her long-term thinking turned to "short-term" thinking. Suddenly, her stock plan that had averaged 15% per year and had grown to over $600,000 did not look as attractive an investment as rental property paying monthly rent, but averaging much less in over-all returns.

Lets look at the "losses" from moving this money from a "higher paying" investment to a "lower-paying" investment:

A) Money: She has about $ 300,000 less now than she would have had if the money was left in the stock fund, and was not used to buy rental property.

B) TIME: In how many years can she make up this difference? About two years? (That's about what stock fund can be expected to generate over two years?) The correct answer is "NEVER."

Those two years are lost. No interest can ever be made from them! We have lost the use of those two years, and cannot get it back.

Now, I don't want anyone feeling sorry for my "long lost friend." A few months ago she decided to retire. Said she just doesn't want to go to work anymore. She certainly has enough money to retire. (And, retiring from an airline means she will fly free for the rest of her life!) She doesn't have the million yet, but she should get there in a few years. (Most of us won't make it that far; we will find something else to do before we get there.) She kept the rental property, and will try to live on the rental income that it generates. She has sold about half of her stock fund and replaced it with no-load mutual funds that expect to earn 14 to 16% per year. She is going to let the interest build up until she has her million dollars. She may even get there before I do! And remember, she had to borrow $200 from me to get started! (I am still writing this book!) Well, she is having fun and doing what she wants to do. And, she really could have done it a couple of years ago. She certainly had enough money to "buy a couple of years!"

Case Two: Office Worker (Aunt Lucy)

Aunt Lucy had decided that she would like to retire at age 62, and wanted some extra money to play golf several times each week. So, at age 55 Aunt Lucy started putting money into a tax-deferred retirement plan: $5,000 each year into a bank CD with a rate of 8%. Here is the chartwork:

YEARS	Aunt Lucy's Age	Accumulated Total @ 8%	Interest Payout @8%/Year	Interest Per Month
15	69	$146,621	$11,729	$977
14	68	130,760	10,460	871
13	67	116,476	9,285	773
12	66	102,885	8,539	711
11	65	89,885	7,190	599
10	64	78,227	6,258	521
9	63	67,432	5,394	449
8	**62**	**57,437**	**4,594**	**382**
7	61	48,183	3,854	321
6	60	39,814	3,185	265
5	59	31,679	2,534	211
4	58	24,233		
3	57	17,530		
2	56	11,232		
1	55	5,400		

Social Security covered most of her bills, but she still couldn't play as much golf as she wanted to. Her retirement fund had only $57,437 and gave her only $4,594/yr ($382/ month) to play golf on. This was not enough money. Aunt Lucy worked several more years until she had enough money to play golf.

What could Aunt Lucy have done differently?

A) MONEY: Invest more money? No. Not an option in this case. The $5,000 per year is as much as Aunt Lucy can afford to invest.

B) TIME: Maybe if there had been more time to think about retirement, Aunt Lucy could have started investing sooner–say at age 50. Then she would have all the amounts on the above table 5 years sooner. She would have $57,437 by age 57 instead of at age 62. And at age of 62 she would have had $116,074 and been able to retire and play golf instead of waiting till age 67. If she had started putting away money at age 47, she would have everything on the above table 8 years earlier, and enough TIME and MONEY to play golf.

C) INTEREST:_Aunt Lucy settled for an 8% CD from a local bank. Could she have done better than this 8%? At that time, there were many no-load mutual funds paying in the high teens and low 20's. Aunt Lucy could have easily gotten 10,12, or 14 % interest (*and probably even more*) for this period with little risk.

YEARS	10% Interest	12% Interest	14% Interest
15	$174,748	208,566	249,901
14	153,862	181,198	214,212
13	134,874	156,762	182,905
12	117,613	134,945	155,443
11	101,921	115,465	131,353
10	87,655	98,072	110,222
9	74,687	82,543	91,686
8	**62,897**	**68,878**	**75,426**
7	52,179	56,498	61,163
6	42,435	45,445	48,652
5	33,578	35,575	37,677
4	25,525	26,764	28,050
3	18,205	18,896	19,605
2	11,550	11,872	12,198
1	5,500	5,600	5,700

Of course, these higher interest rates are not possible if you don't know about them, and where to find them. Aunt Lucy didn't know! Here is the income these higher rates of interest would produce:

Year	10% Year	Month	12% Year	Month	14% Year	Month
15	$17,474	$1,456	$25,027	$2,085	$34,986	$2,915
14	15,386	1,282	21,743	1,811	29,989	2,499
13	13,487	1,123	18,811	1,567	25,606	2,133
12	11,761	980	16,193	1,349	21,762	1,813
11	10,192	849	13,855	1,154	18,389	1,532
10	8,765	730	11,768	980	15,431	1,285
9	7,468	622	9,905	825	12,836	1,069
8	6,289	524	8,265	688	10,559	879
7	5,217	434	6,779	564	8,562	713
6	4,245	353	5,433	454	6,811	567
5	3,357	279	4,269	355	5,274	439

See how much more Aunt Lucy could have had if she had fully known her choices! She could have had $879 per month interest income at age 62. With that amount she could have played golf! Had she fully realized her retirement and started at age 47, she could have had $2,915 a month in retirement interest income. That can pay for a lot of golf almost anywhere she might want to play!

This case is all too common. Someone retires only to find out that pension and social security are less than they expected. The worst case is that they have to work a few more years to have enough money to retire on. Aunt Lucy didn't have a pension. Social security paid most of the bills, but she didn't have enough money left to have the lifestyle she wanted, so she worked an additional five years. Aunt Lucy failed in two respects:

A). TIME: She didn't start investing soon enough, and lost *five years*. Had she started sooner she would have reached her goals by age 62.

B). INTEREST: Had she looked beyond her local bank; she could have had better interest rates and $600 to $800 per month to play golf–much better than the $380 per month she got at 8%.

C). TIME and INTEREST: By using both of these to her advantage, Aunt Lucy could have almost $3,000 per month to play golf.

Because she didn't plan soon enough; Aunt Lucy was a victim of both TIME and INTEREST and it cost her at least five years. (That is roughly the equivalent of one doubling period. See the tables.)

Case Three: New Restaurant Owner

Larry just opened a new restaurant. It was a great occasion, since he had worked as a cook in other restaurants for several years. He liked running his restaurant the way he thought a restaurant should be run. It was quite different from working for someone else. Larry knew how to prepare the food, serve the customers, and supervise the wait staff. He had done it all before, while working for others.

When it came to giving himself a savings account, Larry worked out a deal with a local bank. Larry got 6% annual interest but had to invest $1,000 each month. The interest, however, was taxable, and Larry received a 1099 from the bank each year reporting the interest. Here are Larry's totals:

Years	Investment	+ Bal	Sub-Total	Interest	- Tax	Balance
1	$ 12,000	0	0	$ 720	($ 216)	$ 12,504
2	12,000	$ 12,504	$ 24,504	1,470	(441)	25,533
3	12,000	25,533	37,553	2,252	(676)	39,109
4	12,000	39,109	51,109	3,067	(920)	59,256
5	12,000	59,256	71,256	4,275	(1,283)	74,248
6	12,000	74,248	86,248	5,175	(1,552)	89,871
7	12,000	89,871	101,871	6,112	(1,834)	106,149
8	12,000	106,149	118,149	7,089	(2,127)	123,111
9	12,000	123,111	135,111	8,107	(2,432)	140,786
10	12,000	$140,786	$152,786	9,167	($2,750)	159,203
Total	$120,000			$39,203		$159,203

After ten years, Larry has invested $120,000 and has received $39,203 in interest. His total amount is $159,203. Had Larry seen his accountant and set up a tax-deferred retirement plan he would have done better:

Years	$2000	$4000	$6000	$8000	$10000
10	$27,942	$55,884	$83,826	$11,1768	$139,710
9	24,360	48,720	73,080	97,440	121,800
8	20,981	41,962	62,943	83,924	104,905
7	17,794	35,588	53,382	71,176	88,970
6	14,787	29,574	44,361	59,148	73,935
5	11,950	23,900	35,850	47,800	59,750
4	9,274	18,548	27,822	37,096	46,370

3	6,749	13,498	20,247	26,996	33,745
2	4,367	8,734	13,101	17,468	21,835
1	2,120	4,240	6,360	8,480	10,600

My tables only go up to $10,000 per year. Yet, even with $2,000 per year less invested and at the same 6% interest rate (why would anyone want 6% interest?) Larry actually would have gotten just a little more interest ($39,710 versus $39,203) than on his bank's savings plan. Lets assume Larry could have invested in some mutual funds averaging 8% interest (8% still isn't very good!)

Years	$2000	$4000	$6000	$8000	$10000
10	$31,290	$62,580	$93,870	$125,160	$156,450
9	26,973	53,946	80,919	107,892	134,865
8	22,975	45,950	68,925	91,900	114,875
7	19,273	38,546	57,819	77,092	96,365
6	15,845	31,690	47,535	63,380	79,225
5	12,671	25,342	38,013	50,684	63,355
4	9,733	19,466	29,199	38,932	48,665
3	7,012	14,024	21,036	28,048	35,060
2	4,492	8,984	13,476	17,968	22,460
1	2,160	4,320	6,480	8,640	10,800

Even with a lousy interest rate of 8% Larry gets $56,450 in interest for those 10 years. That is better than the $39,203 that the bank wants to give him. Now lets assume that Larry picked out a few good mutual funds and averaged 14%.

Years	$2000	$4000	$6000	$8000	$10000
10	$44,089	$88,178	$132,267	$176,356	$220,445
9	36,674	73,348	110,022	146,696	183,370
8	30,170	60,340	90,510	120,680	150,850
7	24,465	48,930	73,395	97,860	122,325
6	19,460	38,920	58,380	77,840	97,300
5	15,071	30,142	45,213	60,284	75,355
4	11,220	22,440	33,660	44,880	56,100

3	7,842	15,684	23,526	31,368	39,210
2	4,879	9,758	14,637	19,516	24,395
1	2,280	4,560	6,840	9,120	11,400

Now Larry is really getting some substantial return on his investment–$120,445 in interest for his 10 years ($220,445 minus $100,000.) This 14% is still well below the market average of 18% for the last 20 years. Suppose we can get Larry up to average:

Years	$2000	$4000	$6000	$8000	$10000
10	$55,510	$111,020	$166,530	$222,040	**$277,550**
9	45,042	90,084	135,126	180,168	225,210
8	36,171	72,342	108,513	144,684	180,855
7	28,653	57,306	85,959	114,612	143,265
6	22,283	44,566	66,849	89,132	111,415
5	16,883	33,766	50,649	67,532	84,415
4	12,308	24,616	36,924	49,232	61,540
3	8,430	16,860	25,290	33,720	42,150
2	5,144	10,288	15,432	20,576	25,720
1	2,360	4,720	7,080	9,440	11,800

So, if Larry had gone to a tax-deferred plan with mutual funds and just achieved the return of the market average (who really wants to be average?) he would earn $177,550 for his $100,000 investment. That sure beats the $39,203 the bank wants to give him for a $120,000 investment. Are you beginning to understand why I don't like banks as investment vehicles?

Case Four: Engineering Students

Joe and Luke are both seniors at a nearby University majoring in engineering. I give them a lot of credit for their effort; they are both working full time and carrying a full class load. I was there once, and I know that it is not an easy job. They have inquired about my new book, and have given me some funny looks when I tell them about FRONT-LOADING their savings/retirement plans. First, I tell them that just a standard IRA deduction of $2000 per year returning only 8% interest can amount to almost a quarter of a million in 30 years.

If the interest rate is a little better–say 12%–you will have over half a million dollars in the same time. If one can put another $2,000 per year into a spousal account, the half million mark is reached in 24 years–and the full MILLION in 30 years. Joe and Luke look at the tables and want to know more. They now believe the way to financial success (and independence) is to put aside as much money as they can and to do it as soon as they can–to get that "nest egg" going and growing as soon as possible!

Right now, as co-op workers, they don't have access to a 401(k) plan, but IRA's or Roth IRA'S are within their reach when they file taxes. However, when they are out of school and working; they will put the maximum into 401(k) plans. They are both looking into the table of 16% return. It is 2% less than market average for last 20 years; and they feel it is a very attainable goal, and at least worth trying for! Six to eight thousand a year when they start working can get them to the half-million mark within 14 years. And they can *double* that in only another *five* years!

Those just coming out of college, and those only a few years in the work force are my target market for ideas about investing and getting your money's worth and your life's worth from the TIME you invest in working for the following reasons:

A) The economy is on a run, jobs are plentiful, and there are a lot of young graduates coming into the workforce.

B) There is still a "thinning of middle management" going on in many corporations as a consequence of mergers, downsizing, and simply replacing older workers with younger, less expensive employees. Many of those coming into the job market in their mid-20s are wondering if technology will replace them in their mid 40s; or, will it come even sooner? What they learn may become obsolete when they are in their late 30s, or even in their early 30s. they can very well see reasons to " live below their means"; and to FRONTLOAD their savings/retirement plans. They may not have as much time in the workforce as the people they are replacing!

Case Five: Restaurant Manager

Bill is the manager of a local "squat and gobble." He has been there for years and has no interest of "moving upward," or doing anything else. He drives a Jaguar, and when not working wears lots of fancy jewelry and clothes. His restaurant chain was started a few years ago by some pig farmers who wanted to convince the country that sausage and gravy aren't just for breakfast anymore. They also have "Kool-aid" and fried baloney sandwiches on the menu.

The pig farmers do offer very good benefits. Most employees take advantage of health insurance, but few take advantage of the savings or life insurance programs offered. The company offers a 401(k) plan with several options. The company stock has grown at 22% for the last three years, but is projected to grow only 16% in the current year.

Other options and projected growth in company 401(k) plan include:

A) International Fund   Projected: 14%
B) Bond Fund   Projected: 8%
C) High-Tech Fund   Projected: 22%
D) Real-Estate Fund   Projected: 8%
E) Indexed-Fund   Projected: 16%

Bill does not participate in the 401(k) plan. He says he doesn't need to and that he has plenty of money. Bill takes home about $1,800 a month after taxes. His rent is $600 a month, and the lease on his Jaguar is $550. Bill eats for free–after all he is the manager of a restaurant. But at about 45 years of age, maybe he should be looking at putting something away for retirement. The 401(k) plan is the only retirement plan the company offers. The only other formal retirement income available to employees is their Social Security benefits. Remember Aunt Lucy in case two and see Linda in case 7. They waited till their 50s to act upon retirement.

If I were Bill; I'd get a less expensive car, and start putting some money into the 401(k) plan. That 22% is just too much to resist. At that rate, money doubles every 3 1/2 years! I couldn't resist that rate unless I could do better. How about you? How does 22% interest sound? It sure beats Social Security, Kool-aid, and fried baloney sandwiches! But then, I'd rather have the MILLION DOLLARS than the Jaguar.

Case Six: Server

Sam is a "server" at a restaurant near where I work. (I don't know the difference between a waitress and a "server;" they seem to do pretty much the same thing.) Sometimes I stop for breakfast if I'm not in the mood for Cheerios or Wheaties. It is fun to watch Sam work. When she walks by, heads turn.

Sam is a beautiful woman of middle eastern heritage in her early 30s. She is short with long shiney black hair, big dark brown eyes that turn up at the corners, a big smile with perfect teeth, a perfect complexion, a smooth, soft voice, and a good sense of humor.

Sam's section is always filled. In spite of the uniform of white blouse, black skirt and apron, she is so attractive that you must wait to get into Sam's section.

Sam has been there for several years. She is divorced from a former manager. Sam has talked money with me–investments, retirement, savings–but only on a casual basis. I am not sure she knows what a cost analysis is or does. She admitted to making about $40,000 to $45,000 a year. (As I said, her section is always full!) Sam likes big cars and fancy clothes.

Sam had put money into her company's 403K plan. But after a few years; she took it out for a down payment on a new big car.

Here is part of the plan that Sam looked at:

Years	$2,000/yr.	$4,000/yr.
3	$7,282	$14,564
2	4,620	9,240
1	2,200	4,400

Sam's plan for her savings was to save up a down payment for a new car. She did not look beyond what her returns and growth could have been beyond three years or so.

Here's what that same 10% rate of interest would generate over several years, rather than just the short term that Sam was looking at. At these rates; she could pay cash for new car and have plenty left over to begin a serious savings/retirement plan. With her income level, she could probably put aside more money and at better interest rates than we show here. See Case 7.

Years	$2,000	$4,000	$6,000
15	$70,350	$140,700	$211,050
14	61,996	123,992	185,988
13	54,401	108,802	163,203
12	47,496	94,992	142,488
11	41,219	82,438	123,657
10	35,513	71,026	106,539
9	30,326	60,652	90,978
8	**25,610**	**51,220**	**76,830**
7	21,323	42,646	63,969
6	17,425	34,850	52,275
5	13,882	27,764	41,646
4	10,661	21,322	31,983
3	7,282	14,564	21,846
2	4,620	9,240	13,860
1	2,200	4,400	6,600

Since Sam is in her early thirties, She has plenty of time to invest. But check the table above: she has been at her job 8 years; she could easily have $85,000 to $150,000 in savings by now. And she still has plenty of time to make a lot more money. Maybe after reading this case, she will read the higher numbers on the tables and act accordingly.

Case 7: Waitress

It may be a good sign when people ask you what you can do for them in your new book. Sometimes on weekends I stop for breakfast at a Coney Island in the local shopping center. There is a waitress there who we will call "Linda." Linda asked if my new book could help her retire. She will be 50 on her next birthday. (This sounds like Aunt Lucy; see that case study. Aunt Lucy didn't start thinking about retirement till age 55. At least she didn't start putting money away for retirement till 55.) Here we have an extra 5 years to work with. We also have a little more money; Linda can put away $7,000 per year. There is no tax deferred retirement plan where Linda works. So we will go for a tax-deferred $2,000/yr. IRA. The additional $5,000 will go into high-interest mutual funds, but we will have to pay taxes on any capital gains distributions. Our goals will be 16% return on investment for the IRA's, and 11% return after taxes for the other investments ($5,000/yr.)

Year	$2000 @ 16%	$5000 @ 11%	Total	Principal	INTEREST	Linda's Age
12	$71,572	$126,058	$197,630	$84,000	$113,630	62
11	59,700	108,565	168,265	77,000	91,265	61
10	49,465	92,807	142,272	70,000	72,272	60
9	40,642	78,610	119,252	63,000	56,252	59
8	33,037	65,819	98,856	56,000	42,856	58
7	26,480	54,297	80,777	49,000	31,777	57
6	20,827	43,916	64,743	42,000	22,743	56
5	15,954	34,564	50,518	35,000	16,518	55
4	11,574	26,139	37,893	28,000	9,893	54
3	8,132	18,548	26,680	21,000	5,680	53
2	5,011	11,710	16,721	14,000	2,721	52
1	2,320	5,550	7,970	7,000	900	51

Aunt Lucy had about $54,000 in her retirement fund at age 62, and had to work a few more years. Linda has a total of almost $200,000 in her retirement fund. Linda may not be through yet. Her $2,000 IRA doesn't require any money be removed until age 70.5. If Linda has income, she can still put more money into the fund, and she still collects interest on the account!

Linda's Age	Interest @ 16%
62	71,572
63	83,027
64	96,311
65	111,721
66	129,596
67	150,331
68	174,385
69	202,286
70	234,652
71	$272,196

Note that Linda gets a late start, and can still run a standard $2,000-a-year deductible IRA into over a quarter million dollar investment. and Linda is not through yet! The disbursements from her retirement fund can be made over the several years of Linda's life expectancy. We expect Linda to live to about age 84. That means 13 more years during which to collect interest and to disburse those funds! And Linda didn't start until age 50!

Now, let's suppose that Linda is well and healthy at 71, and has lived on her interest on the 11% fund and Social Security, and has not touched her IRA. Now Linda must begin taking the money out. The minimum withdrawal is 1 divided by remaining years of life expectancy. We expect Linda to live to about 84. That is 14 more years, so in the first year we must take out 1/14th of the balance. But we still get INTEREST on the money remaining in the account. (And, by now, I bet Linda is reinvesting some of the money she is required to take out of her IRA, so; it is still gaining interest in other accounts and funds!)

Linda's Age	Begin Balance	Distribution	Distribution Amt.	+16% Interest	End Balance
71	$272,196	1/14th	$ 19,442	$40,440	$293,194
72	293,194	1/13th	22,553	43,302	313,943
73	313,943	1/12th	26,161	46,045	333,827
74	333,827	1/11th	30,347	48,556	352,036
75	352,036	1/10th	35,203	50,693	367,526
76	367,526	1/9th	40,836	52,270	378,960
77	378,960	1/8th	47,370	53,054	384,644
78	384,644	1/7th	54,949	52,751	382,446
79	382,446	1/6th	63,741	50,992	369,697
80	369,697	1/5th	73,939	47,321	343,079
81	343,079	1/4th	85,769	41,169	298,479

82	298,479	1/3rd	99,493	31,837	230,823
83	230,823	1/2nd	115,411	18,4654	133,877
84	133,877	all	$133,877	None	None
TOTAL			**849,091**		

Since retirement age of 62, Linda's out-take on these two retirement funds is almost ONE MILLION DOLLARS– $960,000 to be exact! Maybe she has put some of these distributions into other interest-bearing accounts and gotten over $40,000 in interest. Then her distributions are over a MILLION DOLLARS. And she didn't start until age 50!

I know some of you believe we are "cheating" to say Linda made a million dollars on her retirement accounts. At any given time, Linda never reached the level of a MILLION DOLLARS in her investment accounts. She did not become a millionaire. However; She did make over a MILLION DOLLARS over the span of her retirement investments. That is a lot better to look forward to than having to live on Social Security alone!

Linda has a PLAN. That plan includes financial security!

Case Eight: A 42-Year-Old Procrastinator

Dan is 42 years old, and works full-time for a major retailer. I've known Dan for 10 years. He puts no money into his company's 401(k) plan and has never opted for an IRA when he does his taxes. He responds that he doesn't want the government getting into his money. My response is: "What money?" Dan puts money into a non-interest bearing checking account and keeps that balance high enough to pay his bills for the next 6 to 8 months. Dan's weakness is model trains. He has a collection of several hundred Lionel and other "O" gauge trains.

Dan has no transformer or track, so these trains never get run to see how well they work. He also collects "G" scale. It's about twice as big as "O' scale. He has only a few dozen of these, but he has track and transformer for this size. He tries to tell me that this is his investment. I can buy into that because most of the items do increase in value over time. The problem may be how long it may take to find a buyer to convert an item back into cash. I have another problem too: "Do these item increase in value as fast as mutual funds?" A locomotive may appreciate in value 30% over 10 years. A mutual fund should do that in less than 3 years!

Dan always procrastinates that he will get around to doing something about his retirement savings. After all, he says, he has plenty of time. Dan has already lost 10 years worth of time. At 12% interest, here is how 20 years of investing will turn out:

Years	$2000	$4000	$6000	$8000	$10,000
20	**$161,397**	**$322,794**	$484,191	$645,588	$806,985
19	142,104	284,208	426,312	568,416	710,520
18	124,879	249,758	374,637	499,516	624,395
17	109,499	218,998	328,497	437,996	547,495
16	95,767	191,534	287,301	383,068	478,835
15	83,506	167,012	250,518	334,024	417,530
14	72,559	145,118	217,677	290,236	362,795
13	62,785	125,570	188,355	251,140	313,925
12	54,058	108,116	162,174	216,232	270,290
11	46,266	92,532	138,798	185,064	231,330
10	**39,309**	**78,618**	117,927	157,236	196,545
9	33,097	66,194	99,291	132,388	165,485
8	27,551	55,102	82,653	110,204	137,755
7	22,599	45,198	67,797	90,396	112,995
6	18,178	36,356	54,534	72,712	90,890

5	14,230	28,460	42,690	56,920	71,150
4	10,705	21,410	32,115	42,820	53,525
3	7,558	15,116	22,674	30,232	37,790
2	4,748	9,496	14,244	18,992	23,740
1	2,240	4,480	6,720	8,960	11,200

Many of you would say that Dan could have $39,309 in an IRA by now. Or if he had put 4,000 per year into a 401(k) @ 12% he would have $78,618 in that account. Had he done both, he would have a total of $107,927. And, at 42 he has several years for this to add interest.

I look at this a little differently from most of you. Dan would have $107,927 today--but he would have the potential of having $484,191 in another ten years (at age 52!) ($161,397 + $322,794)

Right now, Dan's potential is $107,927 in ten years at 12%. And to reach that $484,191 in 20 years! Dan can never recapture that potential Those 10 Years can never be made up. TIME is the single most important part of the savings/investing equation. Dan did have a choice: To have a savings/retirement accounts of:

A) "I'll get around to it!"

or:

B) $107,927 in accounts started 10 years ago.

We have just looked at 10 and 20 years--Suppose Dan works to age 62:

Years	2000	4000	6000
30	**$540,585**	**$108,117**	$1,621,755
29	480,665	961,330	1,441,995
28	427,165	854,330	1,281,495
27	379,397	758,794	1,138,191
26	336,748	673,496	1,010,244
25	298,667	597,334	896,001
24	264,667	529,334	794,001
23	234,310	468,620	702,930
22	207,205	414,410	621,615
21	183,005	366,010	549,015
20	**161,397**	**322,794**	484,191

Dan was well within the range of making a million if he had chosen to do so. He still can, by working until he is 72, or by Investing more and/or by getting better INTEREST rates! He can still make it—even with the ten-year TIME penalty he imposed on himself!

Like Dan, I collect model trains. I like those little brass models of steam locomotives in both "N" scale and "Z" scale. These are 160th and 220th actual size. But my first economic priority is to get the maximum into my 401(k) and my IRA's. Lost TIME in these accounts cannot be made up!

Dan could buy a lot of trains with $484,000 or more.

Case Nine: Engineer

Jim is a young engineer, 26 years old and just out of school. He is right now in his first job after graduation. I talked with Jim about my own plans to retire early. He wants to know more. He will be married soon, so it's not too soon to start putting some money into a retirement/savings fund. His big item is saving money for a house. Jim and his future wife believe they can put aside $4,000 to $8,000 per year between them for a savings/retirement account.

Jim wants not less than 10% interest on these investments. That should not be difficult:

	$4000/yr.	$6,000/yr.	$8,000/yr.
Year 20	$252,912	$379,368	$505,824
Year 19	226,002	339,003	452,004
Year 18	201,538	302,307	403,076
Year 17	179,298	268,947	358,596
Year 16	159,080	238,620	318,160
Year 15	140,700	211,050	281,400
Year 14	123,992	185,988	247,984
Year 13	108,802	163,203	217,604
Year 12	94,992	142,488	189,984
Year 11	82,438	123,657	164,876
Year 10	71,026	106,539	142,052
Year 9	60,652	90,978	121,304
Year 8	51,220	76,830	102,440
Year 7	42,646	63,969	85,292
Year 6	34,850	52,275	69,700
Year 5	27,764	41,646	55,528
Year 4	21,322	31,983	42,644
Year 3	14,564	21,846	29,128
Year 2	9,240	13,860	18,480
Year 1	4,400	6,600	8,800

It sort of got Jim's attention that $8,000 each year at only 10% interest will give him a half million dollars in 20 years! I told him that he would probably sell the house and retire in 20 years (at age 46.) I think Jim can do better than 10%. Let's see how 14% works out. It is still less than the market average of 18% for last 20 years:

Years	$2,000/yr.	$4,000/yr.	$6,000/yr.	$8,000/yr.
20	$207,536	$415,072	$622,608	$830,144
19	180,049	360,098	**540,147**	720,196
18	155,938	311,876	467,814	623,752
17	134,788	269,576	404,364	**539,152**
16	116,235	232,470	348,705	464,940
15	99,960	199,920	299,880	399,840
14	85,684	171,368	257,052	342,736
13	73,162	146,324	219,486	292,648
12	62,177	124,354	186,531	248,708
11	52,541	105,082	157,623	210,164
10	44,089	88,178	132,267	176,356
9	36,674	73,348	110,022	146,696
8	30,170	60,340	90,510	120,680
7	24,465	48,930	73,395	97,860
6	19,460	38,920	58,380	77,840
5	15,071	30,142	45,213	60,284
4	11,220	22,440	33,660	44,880
3	7,842	15,684	23,526	31,368
2	4,879	9,758	14,637	19,516
1	2,280	4,560	6,840	9,120

Well, Jim, just a few more points in interest rate and you can have your half-million in just 17 years instead of 20! In fact, you can even invest $2,000 less per year ($6,000 per year rather than $8,000 per year) and still reach the half-million mark in 19 years.

And if you still want to go for the full million, it's only 22 years away at $8,000/yr. and 14% interest. Jim, his head turning a little bit to jelly, is undergoing a little bit of a shock to discover that he really can become a MILLION-AIRE! It really is within his reach! So far, I've been quoting Jim at less than the actual performance of the market. Let's assume that the market will continue at its 18% pace for another 20 years. Here's how it looks at 18%:

Year	$2,000/yr.	$4,000/yr.	$6,000/yr.	$8,000/yr.
20	$346,042	$692,084	**$1,038,126**	$1,384,168
19	291,255	**582,510**	873,765	**1,165,020**
18	244,827	489,654	734,481	979,308
17	205,480	410,960	616,440	821,920
16	172,136	344,272	**516,408**	688,544
15	143,878	287,756	431,634	**575,512**
14	119,930	239,860	359,790	479,720
13	99,636	199,272	298,908	398,544
12	82,437	164,874	247,311	329,748
11	67,862	135,724	203,586	271,448
10	55,510	111,020	166,530	222,040
9	45,042	90,084	135,126	180,168
8	36,171	72,342	108,513	144,684
7	28,653	57,306	85,959	114,612
6	22,283	44,566	66,849	89,132
5	16,883	33,766	50,649	67,532
4	12,308	24,616	36,924	49,232
3	8,430	16,860	25,290	33,720
2	5,144	10,288	15,432	20,576
1	2,360	4,720	7,080	9,440

Jim's head is still spinning just a little. Yes, it really is possible that you can become a millionaire in only 19 to 20 years. Retire at 46 with a million. Are you sure that you really want it? It can be done quicker with higher IN-TEREST rates, or by investing more MONEY. The tables in the back of the book will verify this.

Case Ten: Cost Analyst

William is a cost analyst in the automotive/aerospace industry. Fifteen years ago, the company he worked for dropped the company-supported pension plan in favor of an employee-driven 401(k) plan. The employee could put as much as 15% of pre-tax income into this plan and company would match up to 3%.

This was looked at as a benefit both to the employees and to the company.

<u>PRO:</u>

A) Allowed the employee to set aside larger amounts for retirement than would accrue for them under just a company-supported plan. In addition, this money was tax-deferred until it was taken out of the fund. All interest is also tax-deferred. (More MONEY than a company-supported plan!)

B) Costs to the company per individual retirement account would be lower than in a company-supported pension plan. In a company-supported pension plan, the company pays all costs. In a 401(k) plan, the company matches employee contributions only up to 3% of an employees' income.

C) All employees become fully vested in the old company-supported pension plan as of the change to the new 401(k) plan. Example: William became fully vested in the pension plan. He had been there for 4 years, and at his pay level and length of service he would receive $132/month at age 62. If he were to stay with the company for 30 years, he would receive about $800/month.

<u>CON:</u>

A) The 401(k) is an *employee-driven* retirement fund! The company will match whatever the employee contributes–up to a certain percentage of the employee's income. (Or, to a specified limit.) The retirement plan becomes completely voluntary on the part of the employee. Example: The employee puts nothing into the fund; the employer matches this "nothing." So when the employee retires there is nothing in the retirement fund and the employee must live on social security benefits.

William, as a Cost Analyst, was already calculating the value of his 401(k) retirement account, considering that 18% of his total salary would earn 12% interest until age 62. It sort of blew his mind that he could become a millionaire before age 62 simply by putting aside 15% of his salary (18% including Company's contribution) each year at a 12% rate of interest! (This is not a high rate of interest!) And, in addition, he got a tax break for doing it!

Case Eleven: Security Guard

The case studies I present in this book fall into two basic categories:

A) Those who don't know that they possess the cash flows and resources to become a millionaire or financially independent.

B) Those who do have the cash flows to easily become a millionaire, and somehow find ways *not* to become one! (For examples, see the lottery jackpot winners, the restaurant with sales in the millions each year, and this case.)

Tim worked as a security guard. Several years ago his mother died in a hospital as a result of being given the wrong medication. The insurance company for the hospital had settled out of court. After expenses, a total of 3.2 million dollars was divided between Tim, his brother and his two sisters ($800,000 each.) I saw the four of them in a restaurant arguing about what to do with the money.

Tim's brother-in-law wanted Tim to invest his share in the brother-in-law's company. He promised a better return than Tim could get in a bank. Tim had once lent some money to his brother-in-law, never saw any of it returned, and simply didn't trust him. Tim talked to the bank. Isn't that where you go when you want to keep money safe?

He told me, "The bank said a million dollars is worth $45,000 a year." Until he knows what he wants to do, the bank may be the safest place for the money. Better the bank than his brother-in-law!

Note that the bank Tim talks about is only offering 4.5% interest a year! My tables go as low as 6%. But who would want 6% interest? There are so many better investments around, if you know about them! Tim will get $36,000 interest per year. He could easily get $50,000 to $80,000 or more per year. Right now, he just doesn't know. I'll give Tim a copy of this book when it is published.

63

Case Twelve: Lottery Winner #1

(A note about lottery winners: The author is in a special position to know several lottery winners. He is the author of "THE LOTTERY SOLUTION," an analytical book on lotteries that improves the overall odds of buying a winning ticket by six times. Most of the winners covered in the case studies in this book used the methods outlined in "THE LOTTERY SOLUTION." The FBI has also used the book to police the internet for fraudulent lottery products and scams. THE LOTTERY SOLUTION is available through Rivercross Publishing, Inc., for $19.95 plus postage.)

I met this lottery jackpot winner through a letter in my Post Office mailbox. He was already a lottery jackpot winner via an "Easy pick," and had read my book about lottery methods and odds. If you stop using random selection, the odds do improve. I don't like random selection so I don't use it either for the lottery or for investing.

Anyway, he gave me his phone number and asked me to call him collect. I did: He had already received $240,000 a year for 17 years. He had a large house, several vehicles, and $62,000 in a non-interest-bearing checking account. He wanted my advice on how to invest the $240,000 per year for the last 3 years so he wouldn't have to fall back on social security. I tried to put myself into his shoes and here is what I came up with:

Year 18: Live for one year on the $62,000 in the checking account, and invest the $240,000 @ 8% for 3yrs. That should amount to $302,330

Year 19: Live on $60,000, and invest $180,000 for two years. That should amount to $209,952.

Year 20: Live on $60,000, and invest $190,000 = $194,400
                                          Total $706,682

(Note: The 8% is what is left after 12% minus taxes.)

If we can get 8% after-tax on that $706,682, that amount will earn an income of $56,534.56 per year to live on. The lottery winner confided in me that it would be difficult for him to adjust to living on $60,000 a year. That was only one-fourth of what he was used to. Well, we did forget that he still qualifies for Social Security Benefits. That will add another $10,000 to $15,000 per year.

I think he should really try to make that adjustment to living on $60,000 per year. The other option may be to live entirely on the $10,000 to $15,000 in social security. That would be an even greater adjustment.

I wish he could have called me earlier. I would have recommended that for the first few years: he live on $200,000 and invest $40,000.

After twenty years, here is how his investments would have done:

Year 1 $40,000@8%= $186,438
Year 2 $40,000@8%= $172,628

Year 3 $40,000@8%= $159,840
Year 4 $40,000@8%= $148,000
Year 5 $40,000@8%= <u>$137,037</u>
          TOTAL $803,943

8% Interest on $803,943 is over $60,000/yr. A small investment in each of those first five years would have made this seventeenth year decision a little less stressful. What happens if he had invested $40,000 each year, or $60,000? We can calculate that information from our cumulative tables. By investing $10,000 per year at 8% interest we would earn $ 494,225 in 20 years.

$40,000 per year would yield 4 times as much, or $1,976,900. $60,000 per year would yield 6 times as much, or $2,965,350.

Amazing isn't it? He could have lived very well on $200,000/yr and still had almost 2 million dollars left after 20 years. Or, he might have lived very well on $180,000/yr and been worth almost 3 million after 20 years.

I don't believe many will have much sympathy for this lottery winner having to live on $60,000 to $75,000/yr. After all, he had it all; he just couldn't keep it!

Like 78% of all lottery jackpot winners, this lottery winner used the weight of TIME against himself by *not* using the time period to invest and earn some interest on his money!

Case Thirteen: Lottery Winner #2

A couple of weeks after doing a TV show to promote my lottery book, I received a call from Joe. Joe was president of a lottery club and saw me on TV. He called the producer to get my number. He wanted permission to write a computer program based on my methods. I told him that the newest edition of my book had that computer program on a disk inside the back cover. Joe was a retired math and computer science teacher. His lottery club usually bought at least 80 tickets to each drawing, and he wanted a program to select these 80 tickets based on a very limited set of parameters. The program in my book would not have selected 80 tickets at a time. However, I had an experimental program that would select as many tickets as he wanted. I duplicated it and sent Joe a copy.

Joe's lottery club members were mostly retirees with good pensions and retirement benefits. The lottery club was a hobby for these mostly well-off retirees. Joe had tried several of the so-called "lottery products" being sold by several scam-artists. One can get more winners by picking numbers from a hat than by using their expensive books, software, and schemes. Fortunately the FBI has rid the internet of most of them.

Joe's club started getting winning tickets. Four of the winning numbers were occurring about every 170 tickets, and 5 of the winning numbers every 1100 tickets. They were getting two to three winning tickets per month for their 320 or more tickets. Soon, this lottery club was doing so well they had their own lottery terminal!

Club members started using these same methods to buy their own tickets–independent of the lottery club. Well, it happened! One of the members hit a big jackpot on his tickets. Marc will get over a million dollars a year after taxes for several years. His plans for the money are: 1/3 to the lottery club, 1/3 to savings, and 1/3 to his family. Marc has said he will have no trouble living for 5 or 6 years on just the 1/3 that he kept out the first year. Marc bought a new house and two new vehicles and he is making payments on all of them. (He did not pay cash.) Marc and his family are not changed by the lottery money.

Marc has told me, however, that Joe's lottery club will win a jackpot on its own. Marc has made it possible for the lottery club to be in the black for at least the next 20 years. As for that 1/3 that Marc is investing, no money is going to banks or treasury bonds. Marc is investing in mutual funds and is going after those with minimum returns of 15%, though he said he would like more. "If I'm going to pay taxes on it, I want to make some real money," said Marc. He is investing several hundred thousand dollars each year at good interest rates.

I think it is safe to say that Marc is a MILLIONAIRE–and will remain one all his life!

Case Fourteen: Restaurant Owners #2

Cathy and her husband were part owners of a chain of three restaurants. I was in one with a friend one night and told her where I lived. She told me they had another restaurant just a couple miles from my home, and told me the location of their third restaurant. During the summer, I eat out a lot, since the kitchen is the hottest room in my house. Cathy's Greek/Coney Island is close by. The food was good and it was expensive for a Coney Island.

I saw Cathy there only about half the times I went, and asked her how she had so much time off? The truth was she rotated from restaurant to restaurant, and complained that she had very little time off. She had just gotten back from a long vacation in the Mediterranean and Greece. She said she wouldn't get more time off for another 2 months.

I kidded her that she should have enough money to retire by now. She looked at me askance, but after finding out I was a cost analyst, she asked me how they could improve operations to improve profits. First, I estimated that the three restaurants combined should have annual sales of 4 to 4.5 million dollars, and that profits should be 15 to 18%. Cathy told me I was right on the first and wrong on the second. She told me the profits were split among four owners. Still, that should be profits to each owner in the $100,000 to $150,000 range per year.

She gave me full run to observe each restaurant (and to eat for free.) For a few weeks, I took notes, and then presented what I had found to Cathy. First, I had noticed the kitchens were "wall to wall" people. There were so many that they actually got into each other's way. For example, one guy stood over the hot dog grille and "guarded" it cautiously. "There," I pointed out to Cathy. "Is this guy necessary? If he is not there will these hot dogs get up and walk away? Or, will someone steal them?"

Cathy advised me the "guy" was Carl's youngest son. Carl was one of the owners! Suddenly everything fell into place. The primary purpose of the business was not to make money for the owners. The owners made enough to have a moderately good living, but not to become rich or have a really great retirement. The primary function was to *provide employment* for the kids of the owners!

All of the kids of all four owners were employed by these three restaurants. I did wonder how they could all afford expensive houses in nice neighborhoods. These were $250,000 and $350,000 houses. And the cars were Cadillacs, Lincolns, and Corvettes. Not only did the owners provide jobs, but all the kids had been given expensive houses and expensive luxury cars. They were not paid in the normal pay scales for the jobs they were doing. They were being paid several times more.

The purpose of these businesses wasn't to create wealth for the owners. It was to provide for the owners' extended families. Cathy understood when I pointed this out. Millionaire is not in her future.

Maybe we spoke too soon here? All of the four owners are in their mid-fifties and older. But with incomes in the range of $125,000 to $150,000 per year, and the potential to invest $10,000 to $25,000 per year, we do have the potential to make some serious money outside the restaurant. Cathy is already thinking that if she can invest $20,000 a year at 16% she can buy her own restaurant in ten years and have a lot left over. In her case, the potential for a million still exists and she still has time to make it.

The other three owners see no reason to invest. They have the three restaurants and that is the source of their income. They will continue to own the restaurants and their kids will run them for their parents and give them money. Family members working in the restaurants see no reason for investing and making a fortune on their own. They were given jobs, houses, and cars by their families. Now, they actively compete among themselves to have the biggest house, the most expensive car, the most expensive jewelry, and to take the most expensive vacations. The four owners paid cash for almost everything they bought; however the kids are into the payment game–all their possessions are bought on credit.

Cathy bought lunch at an expensive seafood restaurant. After lunch she asked if I wanted dessert. I declined. Cathy looked back at the menu for the most expensive thing she could find. It was oysters in some kind of sauce covered with caviar at about $50 per dozen. She ordered three dozen. While slurping down the oysters, Cathy commented to me: "Its their money I'm eating." The reason she had to work that day was because one of the kids had taken the day off. I think Cathy will make the million, as long as someone else pays for the oysters!

As for the other owners, they are satisfied with the status quo. As for the kids, they will have to change their lifestyles to invest more, and to pay less interest on their purchases. Most people become millionaires by receiving interest rather than by paying interest! These kids seem more interested in paying interest than in receiving it.

Case Fifteen: This is your Case

You have read these case studies about people and circumstances I know about. Now we come to the most important case of all: yours. And I know nothing about it. It is your case; pick up your pen and write down your goals, hopes, dreams, wishes, and your plans for how to attain them. The next few pages are blank for your story. If you would like me to know about it, contact me at my Post Office Box or by E-mail. I would like to hear from you. After-all, I wrote this book to create at least one million new millionaires and to give financial security to several millions more over the next two decades. Are you one of them?

First we examine our situation: We take a look at were the money comes from, and then look at where the money goes. Yes, it really does flow. Businesses sometimes call this a "Statement of Cash Flows." That concept may be new to many of you, but you can't really make plans until you know where you are and where you want to go. This will show you how your money "flows," allow you to determine how you want it to flow, and allow you to formulate plans and goals.

"Cash Flows"
(How the money comes and goes!)

Comes From	Goes To
1. Employment: Salary, Bonus, Etc.	A. Expenses: Food, clothing, shelter, transportation, taxes, etc.
2. Interest	B. Savings: Money marked to meet future expenses.
3. Dividends	C. Investments: Money marked for long-term growth.
4. Royalties	
5. Other	

Most of us do not have enough income from 1 through 5 to become a millionaire. We must work on the other side of this equation by decreasing A and B, and by increasing C. Notice that increasing C also increases the 1 through 5 side of the equation. (Interest and Dividends!) Fill in the actual numbers for these flows, and it gives you an accurate financial picture of where you are. You can then use it to determine where you want to go; and how to get there. "Millionaire" is really possible!

The "Millionaire," The Psychic, and The Atwood Conclusion

Perhaps I really shouldn't write a conclusion for this book. It is your job, the reader, to go out and use the information presented in this book to improve your economic lot. I could present more and more information–but at some point there is enough information. It is time to act on that information.

Before reading this book, most of you had no idea that becoming financially independent or even becoming a millionaire is really within your reach! You can do it by being yourself–you don't have to start a business, you don't have to be a "service provider" to millionaires. Every lawyer, stockbroker, and insurance salesman I know wishes all his clients were millionaires. The tables will show what you need to invest, what interest rate, and how long it will take. Can it be made any simpler? If you do it, it will happen!

If you don't invest the money, don't invest at the rates shown, or don't invest for the length of time shown, then it won't happen! Right now, the average retiree gets about $16,000 per year in retirement and Social Security benefits. The average retiree also spends about $4,800 per year on prescription medicine not covered by Medicare or insurance. The remainder is about $11,200 per year, or about $930 per month. Can you afford to live on this kind of income, or should you invest something for your retirement?

Retirement is a long time away. Why worry about it till it happens? You have planned every thing in your life (or have tried to!) Why should retirement be any different? In fact you really do have a choice. Do you want to become a millionaire at 40? 45? 65? 80? You really do have choices. Until you read this book you never realized that the opportunity exists for you!

Doubling

How often your investment doubles in value is very important. Most who reach the million level will find that they made about half of their million in the last five to seven years. Look at the cumulative tables to see how fast investment doubles at various interest rates. The rates in this table are based on increases through interest only–no additional investment is made.

Annual Interest Rate	Interest per month	Number of. Months required to double.	Number of. Years required to double.
8%	.0065	107	8 years, 11 months
8.7%	.0070	100	8 years, 4 months
10%	.0080	87	7 years, 3 months
11%	.0088	80	6 years, 8 months
12%	.0095	74	5 years, 8 months
13%	.0103	68	5 years, 6 months
14%	.0110	64	5 years, 4 months
15%	.01175	60	5 years
16%	.0125	56	4 years, 8 months
17%	.0132	53	4 years, 5 months
18%	.01389	51	4 years, 3 months
19%	.01461	48	4 years
20%	.01531	46	3 years, 10 months
21%	.01602	44	3 years, 8 months
22%	.01671	42	3 years, 6 months
23%	.0174	40	3 years, 4 months
24%	.0181	39	3 years, 3 months
25%	.0188	37	3 years, 1 month
26%	.0195	36	3 years

Now let's take a look at how money doubles over these "doubling periods." Note that we are talking about a fixed original investment. No additional monies are added in these examples. The results are "non-cumulative"–everything above the original amount is interest.

Year 1	2,000	4,000	6,000	8,000	10,000
Year 5	4,000	8,000	12,000	16,000	20,000
Year 10	8,000	16,000	24,000	32,000	40,000
Year 15	16,000	32,000	48,000	64,000	80,000

Year 20	32,000	64,000	96,000	128,000	160,000
Year 25	64,000	128,000	192,000	256,000	320,000
Year 30	128,000	256,000	384,000	512,000	640,000
Year 35	$256,000	$512,000	$768,000	$1,024,000	$1,280,000

In the above table, the annual interest rate is 15% (actually 14.8%) and the monthly interest rate is 0.116%. Note that the amounts double every 5 years. If we can get 26% interest, the amounts will double every 3 years! See how the two tables fit together. Remember that your investment will double every 3 to 8 years–even if no additional money is added. It will, of course, double even faster if more money is added!

Calculations on Doubling and Tripling:

Sometimes the best way to calculate how long it will take to double or triple your money is to just plug this equation into your scientific calculator, and just keep trying new numbers till the equation is solved.

For doubling: "one plus interest rate" Y^X "TIME" = 2 times.

Tripling is: "one plus interest rate" Y^X "TIME" = 3 times.

For example, let's see how long it takes to double an investment at, say, 8% return. Let's try $1.08Y^X8 = 1.8509$. No, this won't do it. It must take longer than 8 years. Eight years only gets to 85% more.

Let's try $1.08Y^X8.8 = 1.968$. Closer, but still not double. Let's try nine years: $1.08Y^X9 = 1.999$. OK, I'll concede nine years. We did this by compounding the return yearly. If we change the TIME and compound monthly we will get to the double in eight years eleven months. Look at the table.

How long does it take to double at 25% interest?

$1.25Y^X3.12 = 2.006$ 3.12 years! About 3 years 1½ months.

The Rule of 72:

An easy way to estimate doubling time is to divide 72 by the interest rate. The result is approximate, but close enough to be useful. For example, at an interest rate of 8%, money will double in nine years (72 divided by 8 equals 9.)

You can also figure it the other way. If you need your money to double in six years you will have to find an investment with a return of 12% (72 divided by 6 equals 12.)

How Much Money Have We Invested?

These tables are guidelines for your investing. Non-Cumulative tables represent a one-time investment making the same interest rate over a number of years. These show the results for earning the same rate of return each and every year. Unless you have a contract for a specified rate of return there will be fluctuations and variances in these numbers. For example, you may have an average of 10% after 10 years, yet you may not have earned 10% interest in any of the 10 years. If your earned 8% in five of those years and 12% in the other five years, your total will not be the same as my tables show. Depending on the order in which you earned the various rates, your amount might be somewhat more or less than my tables show.

The tables are averages. There will be some variances for everyone–and those variances will be different. Because I don't know what those variances will be and when they will occur, I use straight-line averages. The Cumulative tables are calculated the same way–except that you add the same amount of money each year.

I chose interest rates from 6% (About the highest rate you can get from a bank!) up to 30%. (Look through the mutual funds listing: you will find several funds in and over the 30% range!) You can settle for 6% if you want it; or you can go for 30% or better!

Here are my reasons for the amounts invested on the tables:

$2,000/yr.	The maximum amount allowed for an IRA.
$4,000/yr.	Two IRAs; or 10% contribution for a 401(k) contribution for someone making $40,000/yr.
$6,000/yr.	15% 401K contribution for someone making 40,000/yr or 10% contribution for a couple making $60,000/yr.
$8,000/yr.	20% for a couple making $40,000/yr. Two IRAs and a 10% 401K contribution for the same couple. You don't have to choose between an IRA and 401K. You can have both!
$10,000/yr.	20% contribution for someone making $50,000/yr.

Other amounts: That is why I show you how to do the calculations for yourself. There may be a couple making $80,000/year and wanting to contribute 20%. That is $16,000 per year. They can calculate the returns, or can come close by adding the totals of $10,000 and $6,000 together. Then they may still want to do a Roth IRA for an additional $4,000 per year. The tables are not exact–again because I don't know how much the variances will be, or when they will occur. But they do make accurate guidelines.

The following table accumulates just the amount of money we have put into a program. It does not include any interest or appreciation of values. Subtracting these amounts from the same lines and columns of other tables will give you the amount of interest that you have gained.

NO INTEREST—INVESTMENT PER YEAR AMOUNTS

Years	$2,000	$4,000	$6,000	$8,000	$10,000
30	$60,000	$120,000	$180,000	$240,000	$300,000
29	58,000	116,000	174,000	232,000	290,000
28	56,000	112,000	168,000	224,000	280,000
27	54,000	108,000	162,000	216,000	270,000
26	52,000	104,000	156,000	208,000	260,000
25	50,000	100,000	150,000	200,000	250,000
24	48,000	96,000	144,000	192,000	240,000
23	46,000	92,000	138,000	184,000	230,000
22	44,000	88,000	132,000	176,000	220,000
21	42,000	84,000	126,000	168,000	210,000
20	40,000	80,000	120,000	160,000	200,000
19	38,000	76,000	114,000	152,000	190,000
18	36,000	72,000	108,000	144,000	180,000
17	34,000	68,000	102,000	136,000	170,000
16	32,000	64,000	96,000	128,000	160,000
15	30,000	60,000	90,000	120,000	150,000
14	28,000	56,000	84,000	112,000	140,000
13	26,000	52,000	78,000	104,000	130,000
12	24,000	48,000	72,000	96,000	120,000
11	22,000	44,000	66,000	88,000	110,000
10	20,000	40,000	60,000	80,000	100,000
9	18,000	36,000	54,000	72,000	90,000
8	16,000	32,000	48,000	64,000	80,000
7	14,000	28,000	42,000	56,000	70,000
6	12,000	24,000	36,000	48,000	60,000
5	10,000	20,000	30,000	40,000	50,000
4	8,000	16,000	24,000	32,000	40,000
3	6,000	12,000	18,000	24,000	30,000
2	4,000	8,000	12,000	16,000	20,000
1	2,000	4,000	6,000	8,000	10,000

Interest at 6% NON-Cumulative

Years	$2,000	$4,000	$6,000	$8,000	$10,000
30	$11,486	$22,972	$34,458	$45,944	$57,430
29	$10,836	$21,672	$32,508	$43,344	$54,180
28	$10,223	$20,446	$30,669	$40,892	$51,115
27	$9,644	$19,288	$28,932	$38,576	$48,220
26	$9,098	$18,196	$27,294	$36,392	$45,490
25	$8,583	$17,166	$25,749	$34,332	$42,915
24	$8,097	$16,194	$24,291	$32,388	$40,485
23	$7,639	$15,278	$22,917	$30,556	$38,195
22	$7,207	$14,414	$21,621	$28,828	$36,035
21	$6,799	$13,598	$20,397	$27,196	$33,995
20	$6,414	$12,828	$19,242	$25,656	$32,070
19	$6,051	$12,102	$18,153	$24,204	$30,255
18	$5,708	$11,416	$17,124	$22,832	$28,540
17	$5,385	$10,770	$16,155	$21,540	$26,925
16	$5,080	$10,160	$15,240	$20,320	$25,400
15	$4,793	$9,586	$14,379	$19,172	$23,965
14	$4,521	$9,042	$13,563	$18,084	$22,605
13	$4,265	$8,530	$12,795	$17,060	$21,325
12	$4,024	$8,048	$12,072	$16,096	$20,120
11	$3,795	$7,590	$11,385	$15,180	$18,975
10	$3,581	$7,162	$10,743	$14,324	$17,905
9	$3,378	$6,756	$10,134	$13,512	$16,890
8	$3,187	$6,374	$9,561	$12,748	$15,935
7	$3,007	$6,014	$9,021	$12,028	$15,035
6	$2,837	$5,674	$8,511	$11,348	$14,185
5	$2,676	$5,352	$8,028	$10,704	$13,380
4	$2,524	$5,048	$7,572	$10,096	$12,620
3	$2,382	$4,764	$7,146	$9,528	$11,910
2	$2,247	$4,494	$6,741	$8,988	$11,235
1	$2,120	$4,240	$6,360	$8,480	$10,600

For example, if you invest $4,000.00 @ 6% for 10 years you will have $7,162.00.

Interest at 8% NON-Cumulative

Year	2000	4000	6000	8000	10000
30	$20,125	$40,250	$60,375	$80,500	$100,625
29	$18,634	$37,268	$55,902	$74,536	$93,170
28	$17,254	$34,508	$51,762	$69,016	$86,270
27	$15,976	$31,952	$47,928	$63,904	$79,880
26	$14,792	$29,584	$44,376	$59,168	$73,960
25	$13,692	$27,384	$41,076	$54,768	$68,460
24	$12,682	$25,364	$38,046	$50,728	$63,410
23	$11,792	$23,584	$35,376	$47,168	$58,960
22	$10,873	$21,746	$32,619	$43,492	$54,365
21	$10,067	$20,134	$30,201	$40,268	$50,335
20	$9,321	$18,642	$27,963	$37,284	$46,605
19	$8,631	$17,262	$25,893	$34,524	$43,155
18	$7,992	$15,984	$23,976	$31,968	$39,960
17	$7,480	$14,960	$22,440	$29,920	$37,400
16	$6,851	$13,702	$20,553	$27,404	$34,255
15	$6,344	$12,688	$19,032	$25,376	$31,720
14	$5,874	$11,748	$17,622	$23,496	$29,370
13	$5,439	$10,878	$16,317	$21,756	$27,195
12	$5,036	$10,072	$15,108	$20,144	$25,180
11	$4,663	$9,326	$13,989	$18,652	$23,315
10	$4,317	$8,634	$12,951	$17,268	$21,585
9	$3,998	$7,996	$11,994	$15,992	$19,990
8	$3,701	$7,402	$11,103	$14,804	$18,505
7	$3,427	$6,854	$10,281	$13,708	$17,135
6	$3,173	$6,346	$9,519	$12,692	$15,865
5	$2,939	$5,878	$8,817	$11,756	$14,695
4	$2,720	$5,440	$8,160	$10,880	$13,600
3	$2,519	$5,038	$7,557	$10,076	$12,595
2	$2,332	$4,664	$6,996	$9,328	$11,660
1	$2,160	$4,320	$6,480	$8,640	$10,800

For example, if you were to invest $4,000.00 for 20 years at 8%, you would have $18,642.00.

Interest at 10% NON-Cumulative

Years	2000	4000	6000	8000	10000
30	$34,898	$69,796	$104,694	$139,592	$174,490
29	$31,726	$63,452	$95,178	$126,904	$158,630
28	$28,841	$57,682	$86,523	$115,364	$144,205
27	$26,219	$52,438	$78,657	$104,876	$131,095
26	$23,836	$47,672	$71,508	$95,344	$119,180
25	$21,669	$43,338	$65,007	$86,676	$108,345
24	$19,699	$39,398	$59,097	$78,796	$98,495
23	$17,908	$35,816	$53,724	$71,632	$89,540
22	$16,280	$32,560	$48,840	$65,120	$81,400
21	$14,800	$29,600	$44,400	$59,200	$74,000
20	$13,454	$26,908	$40,362	$53,816	$67,270
19	$12,231	$24,462	$36,693	$48,924	$61,155
18	$11,119	$22,238	$33,357	$44,476	$55,595
17	$10,108	$20,216	$30,324	$40,432	$50,540
16	$9,189	$18,378	$27,567	$36,756	$45,945
15	$8,354	$16,708	$25,062	$33,416	$41,770
14	$7,594	$15,188	$22,782	$30,376	$37,970
13	$6,904	$13,808	$20,712	$27,616	$34,520
12	$6,276	$12,552	$18,828	$25,104	$31,380
11	$5,706	$11,412	$17,118	$22,824	$28,530
10	$5,187	$10,374	$15,561	$20,748	$25,935
9	$4,715	$9,430	$14,145	$18,860	$23,575
8	$4,287	$8,574	$12,861	$17,148	$21,435
7	$3,897	$7,794	$11,691	$15,588	$19,485
6	$3,543	$7,086	$10,629	$14,172	$17,715
5	$3,221	$6,442	$9,663	$12,884	$16,105
4	$2,928	$5,856	$8,784	$11,712	$14,640
3	$2,662	$5,324	$7,986	$10,648	$13,310
2	$2,420	$4,840	$7,260	$9,680	$12,100
1	$2,200	$4,400	$6,600	$8,800	$11,000

For example, if you were to invest $6,000.00 @14% for 14 years you would have $22,782.00.

Interest at 12% NON-Cumulative

Years	$2,000	$4,000	$6,000	$8,000	$10,000
30	$59,919	$119,838	$179,757	$239,676	$299,595
29	$53,499	$106,998	$160,497	$213,996	$267,495
28	$47,767	$95,534	$143,301	$191,068	$238,835
27	$42,649	$85,298	$127,947	$170,596	$213,245
26	$38,080	$76,160	$114,240	$152,320	$190,400
25	$34,000	$68,000	$102,000	$136,000	$170,000
24	$30,357	$60,714	$91,071	$121,428	$151,785
23	$27,104	$54,208	$81,312	$108,416	$135,520
22	$24,200	$48,400	$72,600	$96,800	$121,000
21	$21,607	$43,214	$64,821	$86,428	$108,035
20	$19,292	$38,584	$57,876	$77,168	$96,460
19	$17,225	$34,450	$51,675	$68,900	$86,125
18	$15,379	$30,758	$46,137	$61,516	$76,895
17	$13,732	$27,464	$41,196	$54,928	$68,660
16	$12,260	$24,520	$36,780	$49,040	$61,300
15	$10,947	$21,894	$32,841	$43,788	$54,735
14	$9,774	$19,548	$29,322	$39,096	$48,870
13	$8,726	$17,452	$26,178	$34,904	$43,630
12	$7,791	$15,582	$23,373	$31,164	$38,955
11	$6,957	$13,914	$20,871	$27,828	$34,785
10	$6,211	$12,422	$18,633	$24,844	$31,055
9	$5,546	$11,092	$16,638	$22,184	$27,730
8	$4,951	$9,902	$14,853	$19,804	$24,755
7	$4,421	$8,842	$13,263	$17,684	$22,105
6	$3,947	$7,894	$11,841	$15,788	$19,735
5	$3,524	$7,048	$10,572	$14,096	$17,620
4	$3,147	$6,294	$9,441	$12,588	$15,735
3	$2,809	$5,618	$8,427	$11,236	$14,045
2	$2,508	$5,016	$7,524	$10,032	$12,540
1	$2,240	$4,480	$6,720	$8,960	$11,200

In this example, if you invest $10,000.00 @12% for 15 years you would have $54,735.00

Interest at 14% NON-Cumulative

Years	$2,000	$4,000	$6,000	$8,000	$10,000
30	$101,900	$203,800	$305,700	$407,600	$509,500
29	$89,386	$178,772	$268,158	$357,544	$446,930
28	$78,408	$156,816	$235,224	$313,632	$392,040
27	$68,779	$137,558	$206,337	$275,116	$343,895
26	$60,333	$120,666	$180,999	$241,332	$301,665
25	$52,923	$105,846	$158,769	$211,692	$264,615
24	$46,424	$92,848	$139,272	$185,696	$232,120
23	$40,723	$81,446	$122,169	$162,892	$203,615
22	$35,722	$71,444	$107,166	$142,888	$178,610
21	$31,335	$62,670	$94,005	$125,340	$156,675
20	$27,486	$54,972	$82,458	$109,944	$137,430
19	$24,111	$48,222	$72,333	$96,444	$120,555
18	$21,150	$42,300	$63,450	$84,600	$105,750
17	$18,552	$37,104	$55,656	$74,208	$92,760
16	$16,274	$32,548	$48,822	$65,096	$81,370
15	$14,275	$28,550	$42,825	$57,100	$71,375
14	$12,522	$25,044	$37,566	$50,088	$62,610
13	$10,984	$21,968	$32,952	$43,936	$54,920
12	$9,635	$19,270	$28,905	$38,540	$48,175
11	$8,452	$16,904	$25,356	$33,808	$42,260
10	$7,414	$14,828	$22,242	$29,656	$37,070
9	$6,503	$13,006	$19,509	$26,012	$32,515
8	$5,705	$11,410	$17,115	$22,820	$28,525
7	$5,004	$10,008	$15,012	$20,016	$25,020
6	$4,389	$8,778	$13,167	$17,556	$21,945
5	$3,850	$7,700	$11,550	$15,400	$19,250
4	$3,377	$6,754	$10,131	$13,508	$16,885
3	$2,963	$5,926	$8,889	$11,852	$14,815
2	$2,599	$5,198	$7,797	$10,396	$12,995
1	$2,280	$4,560	$6,840	$9,120	$11,400

Here, if you invest $6,000.00 at 14% for 30 years, you will have $305,700.00.

Interest at 16% NON-Cumulative

Years	$2,000	$4,000	$6,000	$8,000	$10,000
30	$171,699	$343,398	**$515,097**	$686,796	$858,495
29	$148,017	$296,034	$444,051	$592,068	$740,085
28	$127,600	$255,200	$382,800	**$510,400**	$638,000
27	$110,000	$220,000	$330,000	$440,000	**$550,000**
26	$94,828	$189,656	$284,484	$379,312	$474,140
25	$81,748	$163,496	$245,244	$326,992	$408,740
24	$70,472	$140,944	$211,416	$281,888	$352,360
23	$60,752	$121,504	$182,256	$243,008	$303,760
22	$52,372	$104,744	$157,116	$209,488	$261,860
21	$45,148	$90,296	$135,444	$180,592	$225,740
20	$38,921	$77,842	$116,763	$155,684	$194,605
19	$33,553	$67,106	$100,659	$134,212	$167,765
18	$28,925	$57,850	$86,775	$115,700	$144,625
17	$34,935	$69,870	$104,805	$139,740	$174,675
16	$21,496	$42,992	$64,488	$85,984	$107,480
15	$18,531	$37,062	$55,593	$74,124	$92,655
14	$15,975	$31,950	$47,925	$63,900	$79,875
13	$13,771	$27,542	$41,313	$55,084	$68,855
12	$11,872	$23,744	$35,616	$47,488	$59,360
11	$10,234	$20,468	$30,702	$40,936	$51,170
10	$8,822	$17,644	$26,466	$35,288	$44,110
9	$7,605	$15,210	$22,815	$30,420	$38,025
8	$6,556	$13,112	$19,668	$26,224	$32,780
7	$5,652	$11,304	$16,956	$22,608	$28,260
6	$4,872	$9,744	$14,616	$19,488	$24,360
5	$4,200	$8,400	$12,600	$16,800	$21,000
4	$3,621	$7,242	$10,863	$14,484	$18,105
3	$3,121	$6,242	$9,363	$12,484	$15,605
2	$2,691	$5,382	$8,073	$10,764	$13,455
1	$2,320	$4,640	$6,960	$9,280	$11,600

Here, if you put $6,000.00 into an account earning 16% interest for 20 years, you will have $116,763.00.

Interest at 18% NON-Cumulative

Years	$2,000	$4,000	$6,000	$8,000	$10,000
30	$286,741	**$573,482**	$860,223	**$1,146,964**	$1,433,705
29	$243,001	$486,002	$729,003	$972,004	$1,215,005
28	$205,933	$411,866	$617,799	$823,732	**$1,029,665**
27	$174,519	$349,038	**$523,557**	$698,076	$872,595
26	$147,897	$295,794	$443,691	$591,588	$739,485
25	$125,337	$250,674	$376,011	**$501,348**	$626,685
24	$106,218	$212,436	$318,654	$424,872	**$531,090**
23	$90,015	$180,030	$270,045	$360,060	$450,075
22	$76,284	$152,568	$228,852	$305,136	$381,420
21	$64,647	$129,294	$193,941	$258,588	$323,235
20	$54,786	$109,572	$164,358	$219,144	$273,930
19	$46,428	$92,856	$139,284	$185,712	$232,140
18	$39,346	$78,692	$118,038	$157,384	$196,730
17	$33,344	$66,688	$100,032	$133,376	$166,720
16	$28,258	$56,516	$84,774	$113,032	$141,290
15	$23,947	$47,894	$71,841	$95,788	$119,735
14	$20,294	$40,588	$60,882	$81,176	$101,470
13	$17,198	$34,396	$51,594	$68,792	$85,990
12	$14,575	$29,150	$43,725	$58,300	$72,875
11	$12,351	$24,702	$37,053	$49,404	$61,755
10	$10,467	$20,934	$31,401	$41,868	$52,335
9	$8,870	$17,740	$26,610	$35,480	$44,350
8	$7,517	$15,034	$22,551	$30,068	$37,585
7	$6,370	$12,740	$19,110	$25,480	$31,850
6	$5,399	$10,798	$16,197	$21,596	$26,995
5	$4,575	$9,150	$13,725	$18,300	$22,875
4	$3,877	$7,754	$11,631	$15,508	$19,385
3	$3,286	$6,572	$9,858	$13,144	$16,430
2	$2,784	$5,568	$8,352	$11,136	$13,920
1	$2,360	$4,720	$7,080	$9,440	$11,800

Interest at 20% NON-Cumulative

Years	$2,000	$4,000	$6,000	$8,000	$10,000
30	$474,752	$949,504	$1,424,256	$1,899,008	$2,373,760
29	$395,627	$791,254	**$1,186,881**	$1,582,508	$1,978,135
28	$329,689	$659,378	$989,067	$1,318,756	$1,648,445
27	$274,741	**$549,482**	$824,223	**$1,098,964**	$1,373,705
26	$228,950	$457,900	$686,850	$915,800	**$1,144,750**
25	$190,792	$381,584	**$572,376**	$763,168	$953,960
24	$158,993	$317,986	$476,979	$635,972	$794,965
23	$132,494	$264,988	$397,482	**$529,976**	$662,470
22	$110,412	$220,824	$331,236	$441,648	**$552,060**
21	$92,010	$184,020	$276,030	$368,040	$460,050
20	$76,675	$153,350	$230,025	$306,700	$383,375
19	$63,895	$127,790	$191,685	$255,580	$319,475
18	$53,246	$106,492	$159,738	$212,984	$266,230
17	$44,372	$88,744	$133,116	$177,488	$221,860
16	$36,976	$73,952	$110,928	$147,904	$184,880
15	$30,814	$61,628	$92,442	$123,256	$154,070
14	$25,678	$51,356	$77,034	$102,712	$128,390
13	$21,398	$42,796	$64,194	$85,592	$106,990
12	$17,832	$35,664	$53,496	$71,328	$89,160
11	$14,860	$29,720	$44,580	$59,440	$74,300
10	$12,383	$24,766	$37,149	$49,532	$61,915
9	$10,319	$20,638	$30,957	$41,276	$51,595
8	$8,599	$17,198	$25,797	$34,396	$42,995
7	$7,166	$14,332	$21,498	$28,664	$35,830
6	$5,971	$11,942	$17,913	$23,884	$29,855
5	$4,976	$9,952	$14,928	$19,904	$24,880
4	$4,147	$8,294	$12,441	$16,588	$20,735
3	$3,456	$6,912	$10,368	$13,824	$17,280
2	$2,880	$5,760	$8,640	$11,520	$14,400
1	$2,400	$4,800	$7,200	$9,600	$12,000

Put away $4,000.00 at 20% interest for 27 years and you're more than half way toward a million! You'll get to the million in another 3½ years!

Interest at 22% NON-Cumulative

Years	$2,000	$4,000	$6,000	$8,000	$10,000
30	$779,515	$1,559,030	$2,338,545	$3,118,060	$3,897,575
29	$638,947	$1,277,894	$1,916,841	$2,555,788	$3,194,735
28	**$523,727**	**$1,047,454**	$1,571,181	$2,094,908	$2,618,635
27	$429,284	$858,568	$1,287,852	$1,717,136	$2,146,420
26	$351,872	$703,744	**$1,055,616**	$1,407,488	$1,759,360
25	$288,420	**$576,840**	$865,260	**$1,153,680**	$1,442,100
24	$236,410	$472,820	$709,230	$945,640	**$1,182,050**
23	$193,778	$387,556	**$581,334**	$775,112	$968,890
22	$158,835	$317,670	$476,505	$635,340	$794,175
21	$130,192	$260,384	$390,576	**$520,768**	$650,960
20	$106,715	$213,430	$320,145	$426,860	**$533,575**
19	$87,471	$174,942	$262,413	$349,884	$437,355
18	$71,697	$143,394	$215,091	$286,788	$358,485
17	$58,768	$117,536	$176,304	$235,072	$293,840
16	$48,171	$96,342	$144,513	$192,684	$240,855
15	$39,484	$78,968	$118,452	$157,936	$197,420
14	$32,364	$64,728	$97,092	$129,456	$161,820
13	$26,528	$53,056	$79,584	$106,112	$132,640
12	$21,744	$43,488	$65,232	$86,976	$108,720
11	$17,823	$35,646	$53,469	$71,292	$89,115
10	$14,609	$29,218	$43,827	$58,436	$73,045
9	$11,974	$23,948	$35,922	$47,896	$59,870
8	$9,815	$19,630	$29,445	$39,260	$49,075
7	$8,045	$16,090	$24,135	$32,180	$40,225
6	$6,594	$13,188	$19,782	$26,376	$32,970
5	$5,405	$10,810	$16,215	$21,620	$27,025
4	$4,430	$8,860	$13,290	$17,720	$22,150
3	$3,631	$7,262	$10,893	$14,524	$18,155
2	$2,976	$5,952	$8,928	$11,904	$14,880
1	$2,440	$4,880	$7,320	$9,760	$12,200

Now look at what high interest can do for you. $4,000.00 invested at 22% for 28 years turns out to be a million! Not bad for a $4,000.00 investment.

Interest at 24% NON-Cumulative

Years	$2,000	$4,000	$6,000	$8,000	$10,000
30	$1,269,639	$2,539,278	$3,808,917	$5,078,556	$6,348,195
29	**$1,023,903**	$2,047,806	$3,071,709	$4,095,612	$5,119,515
28	$825,728	$1,651,456	$2,477,184	$3,302,912	$4,128,640
27	$665,909	$1,331,818	$1,997,727	$2,663,636	$3,329,545
26	$537,024	**$1,074,048**	$1,611,072	$2,148,096	$2,685,120
25	$433,083	$866,166	$1,299,249	$1,732,332	$2,165,415
24	$349,261	$698,522	**$1,047,783**	$1,397,044	$1,746,305
23	$281,662	**$563,324**	$844,986	**$1,126,648**	$1,408,310
22	$227,147	$454,294	$681,441	$908,588	**$1,135,735**
21	$183,183	$366,366	**$549,549**	$732,732	$915,915
20	$147,728	$295,456	$443,184	**$590,912**	$738,640
19	$119,135	$238,270	$357,405	$476,540	**$595,675**
18	$96,077	$192,154	$288,231	$384,308	$480,385
17	$77,481	$154,962	$232,443	$309,924	$387,405
16	$62,485	$124,970	$187,455	$249,940	$312,425
15	$50,391	$100,782	$151,173	$201,564	$251,955
14	$40,638	$81,276	$121,914	$162,552	$203,190
13	$32,772	$65,544	$98,316	$131,088	$163,860
12	$26,429	$52,858	$79,287	$105,716	$132,145
11	$21,314	$42,628	$63,942	$85,256	$106,570
10	$17,188	$34,376	$51,564	$68,752	$85,940
9	$13,861	$27,722	$41,583	$55,444	$69,305
8	$11,179	$22,358	$33,537	$44,716	$55,895
7	$9,015	$18,030	$27,045	$36,060	$45,075
6	$7,270	$14,540	$21,810	$29,080	$36,350
5	$5,863	$11,726	$17,589	$23,452	$29,315
4	$4,728	$9,456	$14,184	$18,912	$23,640
3	$3,813	$7,626	$11,439	$15,252	$19,065
2	$3,075	$6,150	$9,225	$12,300	$15,375
1	$2,480	$4,960	$7,440	$9,920	$12,400

How to turn $2,000.00 into a million: Invest it at 24% interest for 29 years. Or settle for half a million in 26 years!

Interest at 26% NON-Cumulative

Years	$2,000	$4,000	$6,000	$8,000	$10,000
30	$2,051,853	$4,103,706	$6,155,559	$8,207,412	$10,259,265
29	$1,628,455	$3,256,910	$4,885,365	$6,513,820	$8,142,275
28	$1,292,424	$2,584,848	$3,877,272	$5,169,696	$6,462,120
27	**$1,025,733**	$2,051,466	$3,077,199	$4,102,932	$5,128,665
26	$814,074	$1,628,148	$2,442,222	$3,256,296	$4,070,370
25	$646,090	$1,292,180	$1,938,270	$2,584,360	$3,230,450
24	**$512,770**	**$1,025,540**	$1,538,310	$2,051,080	$2,563,850
23	$406,960	$813,920	**$1,220,880**	$1,627,840	$2,034,800
22	$322,984	$645,968	$968,952	$1,291,936	$1,614,920
21	$256,337	**$512,674**	$769,011	**$1,025,348**	$1,281,685
20	$203,442	$406,884	**$610,326**	$813,768	**$1,017,210**
19	$161,462	$322,924	$484,386	$645,848	$807,310
18	$128,144	$256,288	$384,432	**$512,576**	$640,720
17	$101,701	$203,402	$305,103	$406,804	**$508,505**
16	$80,715	$161,430	$242,145	$322,860	$403,575
15	$64,060	$128,120	$192,180	$256,240	$320,300
14	$50,841	$101,682	$152,523	$203,364	$254,205
13	$40,350	$80,700	$121,050	$161,400	$201,750
12	$32,024	$64,048	$96,072	$128,096	$160,120
11	$25,415	$50,830	$76,245	$101,660	$127,075
10	$20,171	$40,342	$60,513	$80,684	$100,855
9	$16,009	$32,018	$48,027	$64,036	$80,045
8	$12,705	$25,410	$38,115	$50,820	$63,525
7	$10,083	$20,166	$30,249	$40,332	$50,415
6	$8,003	$16,006	$24,009	$32,012	$40,015
5	$6,351	$12,702	$19,053	$25,404	$31,755
4	$5,040	$10,080	$15,120	$20,160	$25,200
3	$4,000	$8,000	$12,000	$16,000	$20,000
2	$3,175	$6,350	$9,525	$12,700	$15,875
1	$2,520	$5,040	$7,560	$10,080	$12,600

Interest at 28% NON-Cumulative

Years	$2,000	$4,000	$6,000	$8,000	$10,000
30	$3,291,009	$6,582,018	$9,873,027	$13,164,036	$16,455,045
29	$2,571,100	$5,142,200	$7,713,300	$10,284,400	$12,855,500
28	$2,008,672	$4,017,344	$6,026,016	$8,034,688	$10,043,360
27	$1,569,275	$3,138,550	$4,707,825	$6,277,100	$7,846,375
26	**$1,225,996**	$2,451,992	$3,677,988	$4,903,984	$6,129,980
25	$957,809	$1,915,618	$2,873,427	$3,831,236	$4,789,045
24	$748,288	$1,496,576	$2,244,864	$2,993,152	$3,741,440
23	**$584,600**	**$1,169,200**	$1,753,800	$2,338,400	$2,923,000
22	$456,719	$913,438	$1,370,157	$1,826,876	$2,283,595
21	$356,811	$713,622	**$1,070,433**	$1,427,244	$1,784,055
20	$278,759	**$557,518**	$836,277	**$1,115,036**	$1,393,795
19	$217,780	$435,560	$653,340	$871,120	**$1,088,900**
18	$170,141	$340,282	**$510,423**	$680,564	$850,705
17	$132,922	$265,844	$398,766	***$531,688***	$664,610
16	$103,845	$207,690	$311,535	$415,380	***$519,225***
15	$81,129	$162,258	$243,387	$324,516	$405,645
14	$63,382	$126,764	$190,146	$253,528	$316,910
13	$49,517	$99,034	$148,551	$198,068	$247,585
12	$38,685	$77,370	$116,055	$154,740	$193,425
11	$30,223	$60,446	$90,669	$120,892	$151,115
10	$23,611	$47,222	$70,833	$94,444	$118,055
9	$18,446	$36,892	$55,338	$73,784	$92,230
8	$14,411	$28,822	$43,233	$57,644	$72,055
7	$11,258	$22,516	$33,774	$45,032	$56,290
6	$8,796	$17,592	$26,388	$35,184	$43,980
5	$6,871	$13,742	$20,613	$27,484	$34,355
4	$5,368	$10,736	$16,104	$21,472	$26,840
3	$4,194	$8,388	$12,582	$16,776	$20,970
2	$3,276	$6,552	$9,828	$13,104	$16,380
1	$2,560	$5,120	$7,680	$10,240	$12,800

Interest at 30% NON-Cumulative

Years	$2,000	$4,000	$6,000	$8,000	$10,000
30	$5,239,991	$10,479,982	$15,719,973	$20,959,964	$26,199,955
29	$4,030,762	$8,061,524	$12,092,286	$16,123,048	$20,153,810
28	$3,100,586	$6,201,172	$9,301,758	$12,402,344	$15,502,930
27	$2,385,066	$4,770,132	$7,155,198	$9,540,264	$11,925,330
26	$1,834,666	$3,669,332	$5,503,998	$7,338,664	$9,173,330
25	$1,411,282	$2,822,564	$4,233,846	$5,645,128	$7,056,410
24	$1,085,601	$2,171,202	$3,256,803	$4,342,404	$5,428,005
23	$835,078	$1,670,156	$2,505,234	$3,340,312	$4,175,390
22	$642,367	**$1,284,734**	$1,927,101	$2,569,468	$3,211,835
21	**$494,129**	$988,258	$1,482,387	$1,976,516	$2,470,645
20	$380,099	$760,198	**$1,140,297**	$1,520,396	$1,900,495
19	$292,384	**$584,768**	$877,152	**$1,169,536**	$1,461,920
18	$224,910	$449,820	$674,730	$899,640	$1,124,550
17	$173,008	$346,016	**$519,024**	$692,032	$865,040
16	$133,083	$266,166	$399,249	**$532,332**	$665,415
15	$102,371	$204,742	$307,113	$409,484	**$511,855**
14	$78,747	$157,494	$236,241	$314,988	$393,735
13	$60,575	$121,150	$181,725	$242,300	$302,875
12	$46,596	$93,192	$139,788	$186,384	$232,980
11	$35,843	$71,686	$107,529	$143,372	$179,215
10	$27,571	$55,142	$82,713	$110,284	$137,855
9	$21,208	$42,416	$63,624	$84,832	$106,040
8	$16,314	$32,628	$48,942	$65,256	$81,570
7	$12,549	$25,098	$37,647	$50,196	$62,745
6	$9,653	$19,306	$28,959	$38,612	$48,265
5	$7,425	$14,850	$22,275	$29,700	$37,125
4	$5,712	$11,424	$17,136	$22,848	$28,560
3	$4,394	$8,788	$13,182	$17,576	$21,970
2	$3,380	$6,760	$10,140	$13,520	$16,900
1	$2,600	$5,200	$7,800	$10,400	$13,000

30% interest is terrific! It gets you to a million in 18 to 24 years!

These next tables are based on investing the same amount of money every year. So in year 30 you would have invested $60,000.00. But look at the return!

Interest at 6% CUMULATIVE

Years	$2,000	$4,000	$6,000	$8,000	$10,000
30	$175,292	$350,584	$525,876	$701,168	$876,460
29	$163,806	$327,612	$491,418	$655,224	$819,030
28	$152,319	$304,638	$456,957	$609,276	$761,595
27	$141,482	$282,964	$424,446	$565,928	$707,410
26	$131,258	$262,516	$393,774	$525,032	$656,290
25	$121,614	$243,228	$364,842	$486,456	$608,070
24	$112,515	$225,030	$337,545	$450,060	$562,575
23	$103,931	$207,862	$311,793	$415,724	$519,655
22	$95,833	$191,666	$287,499	$383,332	$479,165
21	$88,194	$176,388	$264,582	$352,776	$440,970
20	$80,987	$161,974	$242,961	$323,948	$404,935
19	$74,188	$148,376	$222,564	$296,752	$370,940
18	$67,773	$135,546	$203,319	$271,092	$338,865
17	$61,722	$123,444	$185,166	$246,888	$308,610
16	$56,014	$112,028	$168,042	$224,056	$280,070
15	$50,628	$101,256	$151,884	$202,512	$253,140
14	$45,547	$91,094	$136,641	$182,188	$227,735
13	$40,754	$81,508	$122,262	$163,016	$203,770
12	$36,232	$72,464	$108,696	$144,928	$181,160
11	$31,967	$63,934	$95,901	$127,868	$159,835
10	$27,942	$55,884	$83,826	$111,768	$139,710
9	$24,360	$48,720	$73,080	$97,440	$121,800
8	$20,981	$41,962	$62,943	$83,924	$104,905
7	$17,794	$35,588	$53,382	$71,176	$88,970
6	$14,787	$29,574	$44,361	$59,148	$73,935
5	$11,950	$23,900	$35,850	$47,800	$59,750
4	$9,274	$18,548	$27,822	$37,096	$46,370
3	$6,749	$13,498	$20,247	$26,996	$33,745
2	$4,367	$8,734	$13,101	$17,468	$21,835
1	$2,120	$4,240	$6,360	$8,480	$10,600

8% Interest CUMULATIVE

Years	$2,000	$4,000	$6,000	$8,000	$10,000
30	$244,691	$489,382	$734,073	$978,764	$1,223,455
29	$224,566	$449,132	$673,698	$898,264	$1,122,830
28	$205,931	$411,862	$617,793	$823,724	$1,029,655
27	$188,677	$377,354	$566,031	$754,708	$943,385
26	$172,701	$345,402	$518,103	$690,804	$863,505
25	$157,908	$315,816	$473,724	$631,632	$789,540
24	$144,211	$288,422	$432,633	$576,844	$721,055
23	$131,529	$263,058	$394,587	$526,116	$657,645
22	$119,786	$239,572	$359,358	$479,144	$598,930
21	$108,913	$217,826	$326,739	$435,652	$544,565
20	$98,845	$197,690	$296,535	$395,380	$494,225
19	$89,523	$179,046	$268,569	$358,092	$447,615
18	$80,892	$161,784	$242,676	$323,568	$404,460
17	$72,900	$145,800	$218,700	$291,600	$364,500
16	$65,550	$131,100	$196,650	$262,200	$327,750
15	$58,648	$117,296	$175,944	$234,592	$293,240
14	$52,304	$104,608	$156,912	$209,216	$261,520
13	$46,429	$92,858	$139,287	$185,716	$232,145
12	$40,990	$81,980	$122,970	$163,960	$204,950
11	$35,954	$71,908	$107,862	$143,816	$179,770
10	$31,290	$62,580	$93,870	$125,160	$156,450
9	$26,973	$53,946	$80,919	$107,892	$134,865
8	$22,975	$45,950	$68,925	$91,900	$114,875
7	$19,273	$38,546	$57,819	$77,092	$96,365
6	$15,845	$31,690	$47,535	$63,380	$79,225
5	$12,671	$25,342	$38,013	$50,684	$63,355
4	$9,733	$19,466	$29,199	$38,932	$48,665
3	$7,012	$14,024	$21,036	$28,048	$35,060
2	$4,492	$8,984	$13,476	$17,968	$22,460
1	$2,160	$4,320	$6,480	$8,640	$10,800

In this 8% chart, your million comes in the 28th year.

Interest at 10% CUMULATIVE

Years	$2,000	$4,000	$6,000	$8,000	$10,000
30	$362,337	$724,674	$1,087,011	$1,449,348	$1,811,685
29	$327,439	$654,878	$982,317	$1,309,756	$1,637,195
28	$295,712	$591,424	$887,136	$1,182,848	$1,478,560
27	$266,871	$533,742	$800,613	$1,067,484	$1,334,355
26	$240,651	$481,302	$721,953	$962,604	$1,203,255
25	$216,814	$433,628	$650,442	$867,256	$1,084,070
24	$195,145	$390,290	$585,435	$780,580	$975,725
23	$175,446	$350,892	$526,338	$701,784	$877,230
22	$157,537	$315,074	$472,611	$630,148	$787,685
21	$141,256	$282,512	$423,768	$565,024	$706,280
20	$126,456	$252,912	$379,368	$505,824	$632,280
19	$113,001	$226,002	$339,003	$452,004	$565,005
18	$100,769	$201,538	$302,307	$403,076	$503,845
17	$89,649	$179,298	$268,947	$358,596	$448,245
16	$79,540	$159,080	$238,620	$318,160	$397,700
15	$70,350	$140,700	$211,050	$281,400	$351,750
14	$61,996	$123,992	$185,988	$247,984	$309,980
13	$54,401	$108,802	$163,203	$217,604	$272,005
12	$47,496	$94,992	$142,488	$189,984	$237,480
11	$41,219	$82,438	$123,657	$164,876	$206,095
10	$35,513	$71,026	$106,539	$142,052	$177,565
9	$30,326	$60,652	$90,978	$121,304	$151,630
8	$25,610	$51,220	$76,830	$102,440	$128,050
7	$21,323	$42,646	$63,969	$85,292	$106,615
6	$17,425	$34,850	$52,275	$69,700	$87,125
5	$13,882	$27,764	$41,646	$55,528	$69,410
4	$10,661	$21,322	$31,983	$42,644	$53,305
3	$7,282	$14,564	$21,846	$29,128	$36,410
2	$4,620	$9,240	$13,860	$18,480	$23,100
1	$2,200	$4,400	$6,600	$8,800	$11,000

Interest at 12% CUMULATIVE

Years	$2,000	$4,000	$6,000	$8,000	$10,000
30	$540,585	$1,081,170	$1,621,755	$2,162,340	$2,702,925
29	$480,665	$961,330	$1,441,995	$1,922,660	$2,403,325
28	$427,165	$854,330	$1,281,495	$1,708,660	$2,135,825
27	$379,397	$758,794	$1,138,191	$1,517,588	$1,896,985
26	$336,748	$673,496	$1,010,244	$1,346,992	$1,683,740
25	$298,667	$597,334	$896,001	$1,194,668	$1,493,335
24	$264,667	$529,334	$794,001	$1,058,668	$1,323,335
23	$234,310	$468,620	$702,930	$937,240	$1,171,550
22	$207,205	$414,410	$621,615	$828,820	$1,036,025
21	$183,005	$366,010	$549,015	$732,020	$915,025
20	$161,397	$322,794	$484,191	$645,588	$806,985
19	$142,104	$284,208	$426,312	$568,416	$710,520
18	$124,879	$249,758	$374,637	$499,516	$624,395
17	$109,499	$218,998	$328,497	$437,996	$547,495
16	$95,767	$191,534	$287,301	$383,068	$478,835
15	$83,506	$167,012	$250,518	$334,024	$417,530
14	$72,559	$145,118	$217,677	$290,236	$362,795
13	$62,785	$125,570	$188,355	$251,140	$313,925
12	$54,058	$108,116	$162,174	$216,232	$270,290
11	$46,266	$92,532	$138,798	$185,064	$231,330
10	$39,309	$78,618	$117,927	$157,236	$196,545
9	$33,097	$66,194	$99,291	$132,388	$165,485
8	$27,551	$55,102	$82,653	$110,204	$137,755
7	$22,599	$45,198	$67,797	$90,396	$112,995
6	$18,178	$36,356	$54,534	$72,712	$90,890
5	$14,230	$28,460	$42,690	$56,920	$71,150
4	$10,705	$21,410	$32,115	$42,820	$53,525
3	$7,558	$15,116	$22,674	$30,232	$37,790
2	$4,748	$9,496	$14,244	$18,992	$23,740
1	$2,240	$4,480	$6,720	$8,960	$11,200

Interest at 14% CUMULATIVE

Years	$2,000	$4,000	$6,000	$8,000	$10,000
30	$813,474	$1,626,948	$2,440,422	$3,253,896	$4,067,370
29	$711,573	$1,423,146	$2,134,719	$2,846,292	$3,557,865
28	$622,187	$1,244,374	$1,866,561	$2,488,748	$3,110,935
27	$543,778	$1,087,556	$1,631,334	$2,175,112	$2,718,890
26	$474,998	$949,996	$1,424,994	$1,899,992	$2,374,990
25	$414,665	$829,330	$1,243,995	$1,658,660	$2,073,325
24	$361,741	$723,482	$1,085,223	$1,446,964	$1,808,705
23	$315,317	$630,634	$945,951	$1,261,268	$1,576,585
22	$274,594	$549,188	$823,782	$1,098,376	$1,372,970
21	$238,871	$477,742	$716,613	$955,484	$1,194,355
20	$207,536	$415,072	$622,608	$830,144	$1,037,680
19	$180,049	$360,098	$540,147	$720,196	$900,245
18	$155,938	$311,876	$467,814	$623,752	$779,690
17	$134,788	$269,576	$404,364	$539,152	$673,940
16	$116,235	$232,470	$348,705	$464,940	$581,175
15	$99,960	$199,920	$299,880	$399,840	$499,800
14	$85,684	$171,368	$257,052	$342,736	$428,420
13	$73,162	$146,324	$219,486	$292,648	$365,810
12	$62,177	$124,354	$186,531	$248,708	$310,885
11	$52,541	$105,082	$157,623	$210,164	$262,705
10	$44,089	$88,178	$132,267	$176,356	$220,445
9	$36,674	$73,348	$110,022	$146,696	$183,370
8	$30,170	$60,340	$90,510	$120,680	$150,850
7	$24,465	$48,930	$73,395	$97,860	$122,325
6	$19,460	$38,920	$58,380	$77,840	$97,300
5	$15,071	$30,142	$45,213	$60,284	$75,355
4	$11,220	$22,440	$33,660	$44,880	$56,100
3	$7,842	$15,684	$23,526	$31,368	$39,210
2	$4,879	$9,758	$14,637	$19,516	$24,395
1	$2,280	$4,560	$6,840	$9,120	$11,400

Interest at 16% CUMULATIVE

Years	$2,000	$4,000	$6,000	$8,000	$10,000
30	$1,230,322	$2,460,644	$3,690,966	$4,921,288	$6,151,610
29	$1,058,622	$2,117,244	$3,175,866	$4,234,488	$5,293,110
28	$910,605	$1,821,210	$2,731,815	$3,642,420	$4,553,025
27	$783,004	$1,566,008	$2,349,012	$3,132,016	$3,915,020
26	$673,003	$1,346,006	$2,019,009	$2,692,012	$3,365,015
25	$578,175	$1,156,350	$1,734,525	$2,312,700	$2,890,875
24	$496,427	$992,854	$1,489,281	$1,985,708	$2,482,135
23	$425,954	$851,908	$1,277,862	$1,703,816	$2,129,770
22	$365,201	$730,402	$1,095,603	$1,460,804	$1,826,005
21	$312,829	$625,658	$938,487	$1,251,316	$1,564,145
20	$267,680	$535,360	$803,040	$1,070,720	$1,338,400
19	$228,758	$457,516	$686,274	$915,032	$1,143,790
18	$195,205	$390,410	$585,615	$780,820	$976,025
17	$166,280	$332,560	$498,840	$665,120	$831,400
16	$141,345	$282,690	$424,035	$565,380	$706,725
15	$119,849	$239,698	$359,547	$479,396	$599,245
14	$101,318	$202,636	$303,954	$405,272	$506,590
13	$85,343	$170,686	$256,029	$341,372	$426,715
12	$71,571	$143,142	$214,713	$286,284	$357,855
11	$59,699	$119,398	$179,097	$238,796	$298,495
10	$49,465	$98,930	$148,395	$197,860	$247,325
9	$40,642	$81,284	$121,926	$162,568	$203,210
8	$33,037	$66,074	$99,111	$132,148	$165,185
7	$26,480	$52,960	$79,440	$105,920	$132,400
6	$20,827	$41,654	$62,481	$83,308	$104,135
5	$15,955	$31,910	$47,865	$63,820	$79,775
4	$11,754	$23,508	$35,262	$47,016	$58,770
3	$8,132	$16,264	$24,396	$32,528	$40,660
2	$5,011	$10,022	$15,033	$20,044	$25,055
1	$2,320	$4,640	$6,960	$9,280	$11,600

This is what happens to your standard IRA contribution in 29 years at 16%. There's your million!

Interest at 18% CUMULATIVE

Years	$2,000	$4,000	$6,000	$8,000	$10,000
30	$1,866,637	$3,733,274	$5,599,911	$7,466,548	$9,333,185
29	$1,579,895	$3,159,790	$4,739,685	$6,319,580	$7,899,475
28	$1,336,894	$2,673,788	$4,010,682	$5,347,576	$6,684,470
27	$1,130,961	$2,261,922	$3,392,883	$4,523,844	$5,654,805
26	$956,442	$1,912,884	$2,869,326	$3,825,768	$4,782,210
25	$808,544	$1,617,088	$2,425,632	$3,234,176	$4,042,720
24	$683,206	$1,366,412	$2,049,618	$2,732,824	$3,416,030
23	$576,988	$1,153,976	$1,730,964	$2,307,952	$2,884,940
22	$486,973	$973,946	$1,460,919	$1,947,892	$2,434,865
21	$410,689	$821,378	$1,232,067	$1,642,756	$2,053,445
20	$346,042	$692,084	$1,038,126	$1,384,168	$1,730,210
19	$291,255	$582,510	$873,765	$1,165,020	$1,456,275
18	$244,827	$489,654	$734,481	$979,308	$1,224,135
17	$205,480	$410,960	$616,440	$821,920	$1,027,400
16	$172,136	$344,272	$516,408	$688,544	$860,680
15	$143,878	$287,756	$431,634	$575,512	$719,390
14	$119,930	$239,860	$359,790	$479,720	$599,650
13	$99,636	$199,272	$298,908	$398,544	$498,180
12	$82,437	$164,874	$247,311	$329,748	$412,185
11	$67,862	$135,724	$203,586	$271,448	$339,310
10	$55,510	$111,020	$166,530	$222,040	$277,550
9	$45,042	$90,084	$135,126	$180,168	$225,210
8	$36,171	$72,342	$108,513	$144,684	$180,855
7	$28,653	$57,306	$85,959	$114,612	$143,265
6	$22,283	$44,566	$66,849	$89,132	$111,415
5	$16,883	$33,766	$50,649	$67,532	$84,415
4	$12,308	$24,616	$36,924	$49,232	$61,540
3	$8,430	$16,860	$25,290	$33,720	$42,150
2	$5,144	$10,288	$15,432	$20,576	$25,720
1	$2,360	$4,720	$7,080	$9,440	$11,800

Interest at 20% CUMULATIVE

Years	$2,000	$4,000	$6,000	$8,000	$10,000
30	$2,836,515	$5,673,030	$8,509,545	$11,346,060	$14,182,575
29	$2,361,762	$4,723,524	$7,085,286	$9,447,048	$11,808,810
28	$1,966,135	$3,932,270	$5,898,405	$7,864,540	$9,830,675
27	$1,636,446	$3,272,892	$4,909,338	$6,545,784	$8,182,230
26	$1,361,705	$2,723,410	$4,085,115	$5,446,820	$6,808,525
25	$1,132,754	$2,265,508	$3,398,262	$4,531,016	$5,663,770
24	$941,961	$1,883,922	$2,825,883	$3,767,844	$4,709,805
23	$782,968	$1,565,936	$2,348,904	$3,131,872	$3,914,840
22	$650,473	$1,300,946	$1,951,419	$2,601,892	$3,252,365
21	$540,061	$1,080,122	$1,620,183	$2,160,244	$2,700,305
20	$448,050	$896,100	$1,344,150	$1,792,200	$2,240,250
19	$371,375	$742,750	$1,114,125	$1,485,500	$1,856,875
18	$307,479	$614,958	$922,437	$1,229,916	$1,537,395
17	$254,233	$508,466	$762,699	$1,016,932	$1,271,165
16	$209,860	$419,720	$629,580	$839,440	$1,049,300
15	$172,884	$345,768	$518,652	$691,536	$864,420
14	$142,070	$284,140	$426,210	$568,280	$710,350
13	$116,391	$232,782	$349,173	$465,564	$581,955
12	$94,993	$189,986	$284,979	$379,972	$474,965
11	$77,161	$154,322	$231,483	$308,644	$385,805
10	$62,300	$124,600	$186,900	$249,200	$311,500
9	$49,917	$99,834	$149,751	$199,668	$249,585
8	$39,597	$79,194	$118,791	$158,388	$197,985
7	$30,998	$61,996	$92,994	$123,992	$154,990
6	$23,831	$47,662	$71,493	$95,324	$119,155
5	$17,859	$35,718	$53,577	$71,436	$89,295
4	$12,883	$25,766	$38,649	$51,532	$64,415
3	$8,736	$17,472	$26,208	$34,944	$43,680
2	$5,280	$10,560	$15,840	$21,120	$26,400
1	$2,400	$4,800	$7,200	$9,600	$12,000

Interest at 22% CUMULATIVE

Years	$2,000	$4,000	$6,000	$8,000	$10,000
30	$4,311,678	$8,623,356	$12,935,034	$17,246,712	$21,558,390
29	$3,352,162	$6,704,324	$10,056,486	$13,408,648	$16,760,810
28	$2,893,215	$5,786,430	$8,679,645	$11,572,860	$14,466,075
27	$2,369,487	$4,738,974	$7,108,461	$9,477,948	$11,847,435
26	$1,940,203	$3,880,406	$5,820,609	$7,760,812	$9,701,015
25	$1,588,330	$3,176,660	$4,764,990	$6,353,320	$7,941,650
24	$1,299,910	$2,599,820	$3,899,730	$5,199,640	$6,499,550
23	$1,063,500	$2,127,000	$3,190,500	$4,254,000	$5,317,500
22	$869,721	$1,739,442	$2,609,163	$3,478,884	$4,348,605
21	$710,886	$1,421,772	$2,132,658	$2,843,544	$3,554,430
20	$580,693	$1,161,386	$1,742,079	$2,322,772	$2,903,465
19	$473,978	$947,956	$1,421,934	$1,895,912	$2,369,890
18	$386,507	$773,014	$1,159,521	$1,546,028	$1,932,535
17	$314,809	$629,618	$944,427	$1,259,236	$1,574,045
16	$256,040	$512,080	$768,120	$1,024,160	$1,280,200
15	$207,869	$415,738	$623,607	$831,476	$1,039,345
14	$168,384	$336,768	$505,152	$673,536	$841,920
13	$136,020	$272,040	$408,060	$544,080	$680,100
12	$109,491	$218,982	$328,473	$437,964	$547,455
11	$87,747	$175,494	$263,241	$350,988	$438,735
10	$69,924	$139,848	$209,772	$279,696	$349,620
9	$53,314	$106,628	$159,942	$213,256	$266,570
8	$43,340	$86,680	$130,020	$173,360	$216,700
7	$33,524	$67,048	$100,572	$134,096	$167,620
6	$25,479	$50,958	$76,437	$101,916	$127,395
5	$18,884	$37,768	$56,652	$75,536	$94,420
4	$13,479	$26,958	$40,437	$53,916	$67,395
3	$9,048	$18,096	$27,144	$36,192	$45,240
2	$5,416	$10,832	$16,248	$21,664	$27,080
1	$2,440	$4,880	$7,320	$9,760	$12,200

Interest at 24% CUMULATIVE

Years	$2,000	$4,000	$6,000	$8,000	$10,000
30	$6,568,744	$13,137,488	$19,706,232	$26,274,976	$32,843,720
29	$5,299,104	$10,598,208	$15,897,312	$21,196,416	$26,495,520
28	$4,275,201	$8,550,402	$12,825,603	$17,100,804	$21,376,005
27	$3,419,472	$6,838,944	$10,258,416	$13,677,888	$17,097,360
26	$2,783,562	$5,567,124	$8,350,686	$11,134,248	$13,917,810
25	$2,246,538	$4,493,076	$6,739,614	$8,986,152	$11,232,690
24	$1,813,454	$3,626,908	$5,440,362	$7,253,816	$9,067,270
23	$1,464,193	$2,928,386	$4,392,579	$5,856,772	$7,320,965
22	$1,182,531	$2,365,062	$3,547,593	$4,730,124	$5,912,655
21	$955,384	$1,910,768	$2,866,152	$3,821,536	$4,776,920
20	$772,200	$1,544,400	$2,316,600	$3,088,800	$3,861,000
19	$624,472	$1,248,944	$1,873,416	$2,497,888	$3,122,360
18	$505,336	$1,010,672	$1,516,008	$2,021,344	$2,526,680
17	$409,259	$818,518	$1,227,777	$1,637,036	$2,046,295
16	$313,182	$626,364	$939,546	$1,252,728	$1,565,910
15	$250,697	$501,394	$752,091	$1,002,788	$1,253,485
14	$200,306	$400,612	$600,918	$801,224	$1,001,530
13	$159,667	$319,334	$479,001	$638,668	$798,335
12	$126,895	$253,790	$380,685	$507,580	$634,475
11	$100,465	$200,930	$301,395	$401,860	$502,325
10	$79,151	$158,302	$237,453	$316,604	$395,755
9	$61,962	$123,924	$185,886	$247,848	$309,810
8	$48,100	$96,200	$144,300	$192,400	$240,500
7	$36,921	$73,842	$110,763	$147,684	$184,605
6	$27,384	$54,768	$82,152	$109,536	$136,920
5	$20,114	$40,228	$60,342	$80,456	$100,570
4	$14,251	$28,502	$42,753	$57,004	$71,255
3	$9,368	$18,736	$28,104	$37,472	$46,840
2	$5,555	$11,110	$16,665	$22,220	$27,775
1	$2,480	$4,960	$7,440	$9,920	$12,400

If you can invest $10,000.00 per year for 14 years, you would have put away $140,000.00. At 24%, that gets you to a million!

Interest at 26% CUMULATIVE

Years	$2,000	$4,000	$6,000	$8,000	$10,000
30	$9,933,905	$19,867,810	$29,801,715	$39,735,620	$49,669,525
29	$7,882,051	$15,764,102	$23,646,153	$31,528,204	$39,410,255
28	$6,253,596	$12,507,192	$18,760,788	$25,014,384	$31,267,980
27	$4,961,172	$9,922,344	$14,883,516	$19,844,688	$24,805,860
26	$3,935,438	$7,870,876	$11,806,314	$15,741,752	$19,677,190
25	$3,121,363	$6,242,726	$9,364,089	$12,485,452	$15,606,815
24	$2,475,272	$4,950,544	$7,425,816	$9,901,088	$12,376,360
23	$1,962,502	$3,925,004	$5,887,506	$7,850,008	$9,812,510
22	$1,565,541	$3,131,082	$4,696,623	$6,262,164	$7,827,705
21	$1,232,556	$2,465,112	$3,697,668	$4,930,224	$6,162,780
20	$976,219	$1,952,438	$2,928,657	$3,904,876	$4,881,095
19	$772,777	$1,545,554	$2,318,331	$3,091,108	$3,863,885
18	$611,315	$1,222,630	$1,833,945	$2,445,260	$3,056,575
17	$483,170	$966,340	$1,449,510	$1,932,680	$2,415,850
16	$381,469	$762,938	$1,144,407	$1,525,876	$1,907,345
15	$300,753	$601,506	$902,259	$1,203,012	$1,503,765
14	$236,693	$473,386	$710,079	$946,772	$1,183,465
13	$185,851	$371,702	$557,553	$743,404	$929,255
12	$145,501	$291,002	$436,503	$582,004	$727,505
11	$113,477	$226,954	$340,431	$453,908	$567,385
10	$88,061	$176,122	$264,183	$352,244	$440,305
9	$67,889	$135,778	$203,667	$271,556	$339,445
8	$51,880	$103,760	$155,640	$207,520	$259,400
7	$39,175	$78,350	$117,525	$156,700	$195,875
6	$29,091	$58,182	$87,273	$116,364	$145,455
5	$21,088	$42,176	$63,264	$84,352	$105,440
4	$14,736	$29,472	$44,208	$58,944	$73,680
3	$9,695	$19,390	$29,085	$38,780	$48,475
2	$5,695	$11,390	$17,085	$22,780	$28,475
1	$2,520	$5,040	$7,560	$10,080	$12,600

Interest at 28% CUMULATIVE

Years	$2,000	$4,000	$6,000	$8,000	$10,000
30	$15,035,469	$30,070,938	$45,106,407	$60,141,876	$75,177,345
29	$11,744,460	$23,488,920	$35,233,380	$46,977,840	$58,722,300
28	$9,173,359	$18,346,718	$27,520,077	$36,693,436	$45,866,795
27	$7,164,686	$14,329,372	$21,494,058	$28,658,744	$35,823,430
26	$5,595,411	$11,190,822	$16,786,233	$22,381,644	$27,977,055
25	$4,369,414	$8,738,828	$13,108,242	$17,477,656	$21,847,070
24	$3,411,605	$6,823,210	$10,234,815	$13,646,420	$17,058,025
23	$2,663,316	$5,326,632	$7,989,948	$10,653,264	$13,316,580
22	$2,078,715	$4,157,430	$6,236,145	$8,314,860	$10,393,575
21	$1,621,996	$3,243,992	$4,865,988	$6,487,984	$8,109,980
20	**$1,265,184**	$2,530,368	$3,795,552	$5,060,736	$6,325,920
19	$986,425	$1,972,850	$2,959,275	$3,945,700	$4,932,125
18	$768,644	$1,537,288	$2,305,932	$3,074,576	$3,843,220
17	**$598,503**	**$1,197,006**	$1,795,509	$2,394,012	$2,992,515
16	$465,580	$931,160	$1,396,740	$1,862,320	$2,327,900
15	$361,734	$723,468	**$1,085,202**	$1,446,936	$1,808,670
14	$280,604	**$561,208**	$841,812	**$1,122,416**	$1,403,020
13	$217,222	$434,444	$651,666	$868,888	**$1,086,110**
12	$167,704	$335,408	**$503,112**	$670,816	$838,520
11	$129,019	$258,038	$387,057	**$516,076**	$645,095
10	$98,796	$197,592	$296,388	$395,184	**$493,980**
9	$75,185	$150,370	$225,555	$300,740	$375,925
8	$56,738	$113,476	$170,214	$226,952	$283,690
7	$42,326	$84,652	$126,978	$169,304	$211,630
6	$31,067	$62,134	$93,201	$124,268	$155,335
5	$22,271	$44,542	$66,813	$89,084	$111,355
4	$15,399	$30,798	$46,197	$61,596	$76,995
3	$10,031	$20,062	$30,093	$40,124	$50,155
2	$5,836	$11,672	$17,508	$23,344	$29,180
1	$2,560	$5,120	$7,680	$10,240	$12,800

Interest at 30% CUMULATIVE

Years	$2,000	$4,000	$6,000	$8,000	$10,000
30	$22,697,962	$45,395,924	$68,093,886	$90,791,848	$113,489,810
29	$17,457,970	$34,915,940	$52,373,910	$69,831,880	$87,289,850
28	$13,427,208	$26,854,416	$40,281,624	$53,708,832	$67,136,040
27	$10,326,621	$20,653,242	$30,979,863	$41,306,484	$51,633,105
26	$7,941,555	$15,883,110	$23,824,665	$31,766,220	$39,707,775
25	$6,106,888	$12,213,776	$18,320,664	$24,427,552	$30,534,440
24	$4,695,606	$9,391,212	$14,086,818	$18,782,424	$23,478,030
23	$3,610,005	$7,220,010	$10,830,015	$14,440,020	$18,050,025
22	$2,774,927	$5,549,854	$8,324,781	$11,099,708	$13,874,635
21	$2,132,559	$4,265,118	$6,397,677	$8,530,236	$10,662,795
20	$1,638,430	$3,276,860	$4,915,290	$6,553,720	$8,192,150
19	**$1,258,330**	$2,516,660	$3,774,990	$5,033,320	$6,291,650
18	$965,946	$1,931,892	$2,897,838	$3,863,784	$4,829,730
17	$741,036	$1,482,072	$2,223,108	$2,964,144	$3,705,180
16	**$568,027**	**$1,136,054**	$1,704,081	$2,272,108	$2,840,135
15	$434,944	$869,888	$1,304,832	$1,739,776	$2,174,720
14	$332,572	$665,144	**$997,716**	$1,330,288	$1,662,860
13	$253,825	**$507,650**	$761,475	**$1,015,300**	**$1,269,125**
12	$193,250	$386,500	**$579,750**	$773,000	**$966,250**
11	$146,653	$293,306	$439,959	**$586,612**	$733,265
10	$110,810	$221,620	$332,430	$443,240	**$554,050**
9	$83,238	$166,476	$249,714	$332,952	$416,190
8	$62,029	$124,058	$186,087	$248,116	$310,145
7	$45,715	$91,430	$137,145	$182,860	$228,575
6	$33,165	$66,330	$99,495	$132,660	$165,825
5	$23,512	$47,024	$70,536	$94,048	$117,560
4	$16,086	$32,172	$48,258	$64,344	$80,430
3	$10,374	$20,748	$31,122	$41,496	$51,870
2	$5,980	$11,960	$17,940	$23,920	$29,900
1	$2,600	$5,200	$7,800	$10,400	$13,000

A million in just over 12 years? Yes, if you put away $10,000.00 per year at 30% interest.

"Where Can I get 16% Interest?"

(How about 30% or More)

One of my most-used examples in this book is to invest $2,000 into an IRA @ 16% interest–and in 29 years you will have $1,058,000. At first, some doubt the mathematics but realize I wouldn't give them bad information. Then comes the question: *"Where can I get 16% interest?"* I am getting rather tired of this question. It is like driving a Rolls Royce in a busy intersection. The guy next to you motions to you, so you roll down the window to see what he wants. He tells you that you are driving a great car, but then asks you where he can buy a Ford!

I will answer that question, but not for 16%. My tables end at 30% annual interest, so I'm going to list about 280 mutual funds that have returned 30% *or more* for the last 5 years. Every fund listed equals or tops my highest interest rates. Those who can't find 16% or higher rates probably have not been looking beyond their local bank, credit union, or savings and loan. Even though I am telling you here where to find higher rates of interest, I will still get some letters complaining that they did what I told them–but their bank would only give them 6% interest. (That is not what I told you to do!) In fact, I don't recommend putting more than 20-30% of your savings in any one of these funds. Find a "rock-solid" fund that pays 12-20% interest every year. Then you can look to other funds paying 20 to 25%, and some at 30% or more.

Look for those funds paying dividends and capital gains, and reinvest those payouts. The concept of buying low and selling high works in theory, but ask the many people who bought something and are still waiting for it to go back up to what they paid for it. Buying funds and hoping to sell for a profit short term (just hours or days later) is just a form of gambling. We want to reinvest profits and capital gains to create compound interest on our investments!

Here are about 280 funds that have average gains of 30% or more for the last five years. *They equal or exceed my highest tables!* Names of funds are appreviated in these listings–but where possible we have tried to give the full names of the funds. **n= no load.**

AIM FUNDS A:	Global Aggressive Growth
	Selective Growth Fund
	Summit L Fund
AIM FUND B:	Selective Growth B
AIM GLOBAL THEME:	Telecommunications A
	Telecommunications B

101

ACCESSOR FUNDS:	Growth	
	Small Medium Companies	
ADVANCE CAPITAL:	Equity	n
AETNA CL I:	Growth	
ALGER FUNDS B:	Capital Appreciation	
	Growth B	
	Mid Capital Growth	
ALLIANCE CAP A:	Premier Growth A	
	Technology A	
ALLIANCE CAP C:	Premier Growth C	
	Technology C	
AMER CENTURY:	Growth Inv	n
	Int'l Discovery Inv	n
	Ultra Inv	n
AMER EXPRESS A:	Growth	
	NwD	
AMER EXPRESS B:	Growth	
	StrAg	
AMER EXPRESS Y:	NwD	n
	Growth	n
AMERICAN FUNDS:	Growth	
	NEcoA	
BB&T:	Small Growth Technology	n
BERGER GROUP:	Growth Income	n
	Small Company Growth	n
BLACKROCK INST:	Large Capital Growth L	
	Small Capital Growth L	
BLACKROCK SVC:	Large Capital Growth S	
	Small Capital Growth S	
CHASE FUNDS:	Equity Growth P	
CITIZENS FUNDS:	Citizen Equity Growth S	
	Citizen Global S	
	Citizen Index S	
CG CAP MKT FUNDS:	Large Growth	
DEL INV INST I:	TrendI	n
DELAWARE INVEST A:	DecEIA	
	DelcpA	
	Select Growth A	
	TrendA	
DELAWARE INVEST B:	TrendB	
DELAWARE INVEST C:	Select Growth C	
DEUTSCHE ASSET M INV:	Equity Appreciation	n
DIVERSIFIED FUNDS:	Growth Income	

DREYFUS	Founders Discovery Fund	n
	Growth Fund	n
	Founders Passport Fund	n
	Premier Third Century Z	
EVERGREEN	Aggressive Growth A	
	Omega A	
	Omega B	
EXCELSIOR FUNDS:	Value & Restructuring	n
FEDERATED	Capital Appreciation A	
	Growth Strategies A	
FIDELITY ADVISOR I:	Equity Growth I	n
FIDELITY ADVISOR T:	Equity Growth T	
FIDELITY INVEST:	Aggressive Growth	n
	Export	n
	Growth Companies	n
	Mid Cap	n
	New Millennium	n
	OTC	n
	RetGr	n
FIDELITY SELECTS:	Biotech	
	Broker	
	Computer	
	Developing Communication	
	Electronics	
	Software	
	Technology	
	Telecommunications	
	Utility Growth	
FIRST AMER FDS A:	Medium Capital Growth	
FIRST AMER FDS Y:	International	n
	Technology	n
FLAG INVESTORS	Communications A	
	Communications B	
FORTIS FUNDS:	Capital Growth A	
	Growth A	
FRANKLIN CLASS A:	Capital Growth	
	Equity	
	Small Capital Growth	
FREMONT FUNDS:	US Micro-cap	
GMO TRUST III:	EDC	
	Growth	
GABELLI FUNDS:	Global Growth	n
	Global Telecommunications	n

	Growth	n
GOLDEN OAK FUNDS:	Growth	n
GUARDIAN FUNDS:	Park Avenue A	
	Stock	
HARBOR FUNDS:	Capital Appreciation	
HENLOPEN:	Henlopen	n
HERITAGE FUNDS:	CapAnA	
INDEX FUNDS A:	JCCCAA	
	JCCGlbA	
	JCCGrA	
	JCCGrT	
IDEX FUNDS M:	JCCGlbC	
	JCCGrC	
INVESCO:	Blue Chip Growth	n
	Dynamics	n
	Europe	n
	Small Company Growth	n
	Technology	n
	Telecommunications	n
JANUS:	Enterior	n
	Fund	n
	Growth Income	n
	Mercury	n
	Overseas	n
	Twenty	n
	Venture	n
JANUS ASPEN INSTL:	Aggressive Growth	n
	Growth	n
	International Growth	n
	World Wide Growth	n
JOHN HANCOCK	Large Cap Value A	
	Small Cap Growth A	
	Technology A	
	Large Cap Growth B	
	Small Cap Growth B	
	Small Cap Value B	
:	Technology B	
KEMPER FUNDS	Technology A	
	Technology B	
	Technology C	
LEGG MASON:	Value Trust	
	NavVIT	
LIBERTY STEIN ROE:	Growth Stock	

	Young Investor	
MAS	Mid Cap Growth	n
	Mid Cap Value	n
MFS	Massachusetts Investors Growth A	
	Capital Opportunities	
	Emerging Growth A	
	Growth Opportunities A	
	Large Cap A	
	Medium Cap A	
	Select A	
	Capital Opportunities B	
	Emerging Growth B	
	Massachusetts Investors Growth B	
	International Capital B	
	Medium Capital B	
	Select B	
	Emerging Equity	
MANAGERS FUNDS:	Capital Appreciation	
	Special Equity	
	Mid Cap Growth	
MERIDIAN FUNDS:	Value	
MERRILL LYNCH	Fundamental Growth A	
	Fundamental Growth B	
	Fundamental Growth C	
	Fundamental Growth D	
MONTGOMERY FDS:	Global Communications R	
MORGAN ST DEAN WITTER:	American Opportunities B	
	Developing Growth B	
	Small Company Growth B	
	Equity Growth A	n
NEUBERGER & BERMAN:	Manhattan	
NICHOLAS APPLEGATE:	International Small Growth	n
	Mid Capital	n
	Nicholas A	n
	Nicholas B	n
	Small Capital	n
NORTHERN FUNDS:	Selective Equity	n
NORTHERN INSTL:	Focus Growth A	n
NVEST FUNDS A:	Star Small Cap A	
OAK ASSOC FDS:	Pin Oak Aggressive	n
ONE GROUP:	Mid Cap Growth A	
	Mid Cap Growth B	
	Lg Cap Growth I	n

OPPENHEIMER:	Capital Appreciation A	
	Global Growth	
	Growth A	
OPPENHEIMER C&M:	Capital Appreciation C	
	Global Growth C	
PBHG FUNDS:	Growth	n
PIMCO FUNDS:	Growth A	
	Innovation A	
	Target A	
	Growth C	
	Innovation C	
	Target C	
PACIFIC CAP INST:	Growth Stock	n
PHOENIX-ENGEMANN:	Agressive Growth A	
	Focused Growth A	
	Sm-Mid CapA	
PILGRIM	Int'l Small Growth A	
	World Wide Growth A	
	Mid Cap C	
	Small Cap C	
	World Wide Growth C	
PEFERRED GROUP:	Growth	
	International	
T ROWE PRICE FUNDS:	Int'l Discovery	n
	Science & Technology	n
PROV INV COUNSEL	Growth	n
	Small Cap Fund	n
PRUDENTIAL FDS:	Jennison Growth Z	
PUTNAM FUNDS:	Global Eq	
	Investor A	
	New Opportunities A	
	OTC Emerging Growth A	
	Vista A	
	Voyager A	
	Voyager II	
	Investor B	
	New Opportunities B	
	OTC Emerging Growth B	
	Vista B	
	Voyager B	
	Investor M	
	New Opportunities M	
	OTC Emerging Growth M	

	Vista M	
	Voyager M	
	Global Growth Y	
	New Opportunities Y	
	Voyager Y	
RS FUNDS:	RS Emerging Growth	
RAINIER INV MGT:	Equity	
REYNOLDS FUND:	Blue Chip Growth	n
RYDEX INVESTOR:	Nova	n
	OTC	n
SEI INST STYLE MANAGED:	Lg Growth A	n
	Small Cap Growth A	n
SCUDDER FUNDS:	Global Discovery	n
	Greater Europe Growth	n
	Lg Company Growth	n
SELLIGMAN GROUP:	Cap Fd A	
	Communications A	
	Communications D	
	Global Technologies A	
	Global Technologies D	
SENTINEL GROUP:	Mid Cap Growth A	
SIT FUNDS:	Mid Cap Growth	n
SMITH BARNEY B:	Aggressive Growth B	
SMITH BARNEY L,O,&A:	Aggressive Growth	
SPECTRA:	Spectra	
STANDISH FUNDS:	Small Cap Equity	
STRONG FUNDS:	Growth Inv	n
	Total	n
SUNAMERICA FDS:	Small Company Growth	
TARGET:	Large Cap Growth	n
TCW GALILEO FDS:	Selective Equity	
	Small Capital Growth	
TURNER FUNDS:	Growth Equity	n
	Small Cap	n
UAM FUNDS:	Sirach Special Equity	n
US GLOBAL INVESTORS:	Bonnel Global	n
USAA GROUP:	Agressive Growth	n
UNITED FUNDS:	New Concept	
	Science & Technology	
	Vanguard A	
VAN KAMPEN FUNDS:	EquityGrowth A	
	EquityGrowth B	
	Emerging Growth C	

VANGUARD:	Morg Grow	n
	Primecap	n
	US Growth	n
WM GRP of FDS:	Growth A	
	NWFdA	
	Growth B	
WADDELL & REED:	Growth	
	International Growth	
WABURG PINCUS:	Cap Apppr	n
WEITZ FUNDS:	Hickory	n
WELLS FARGO INSTL:	Long Term Capital Growth	n
WILMINGTON FUNDS:	Large Cap Growth	n
WILSHIRE TARGET FUNDS:	Large Cap Growth	n

Here are about 280 mutual funds that have averaged 30% *or more* for the last five years. There are even more funds paying this much interest; there are many funds not listed. There are probably more than 400 funds that have averaged appreciation of 30% or higher for the past five years. As for those wanting to know where they can get 16% interest; I counted over 800 listed mutual funds that paid between 16% and 29% for the past five years. (Again, there are also some funds in this range that are not listed!) No, I'm not going to list all of those funds–it's four times longer than this list! So for those wanting 16% interest, we offer the following: 280 funds paying 30% interest, plus 800 additional funds paying 16% or better. That's about 1100 funds over 16%. I bet I will still hear the question: *"Where can I get 16% interest?"*